D

WITH

DISCERNMENT

12 QUESTIONS TO MAKE

A LASTING MARRIAGE

Sam A. Andreades

To Veronica and Enoch,
in whom I have the utmost confidence.
I hope that you can enjoy this phase
on your way to a wise decision.

CruciformPress

"**This is a brilliant book!** Much like he did in *enGendered*, Sam A. Andreades has found the sweet spot in reading both Scripture and culture simultaneously to anticipate, articulate, and answer the questions that young people (and their parents) are now asking. He then directs them on how to live faithfully and proactively in the creation ordinance in a post-Obergefell world, where everything from sexual difference to biblical marriage is vexed with Orwellian confusion and despised by those with cultural capital. I especially loved how he opens the book with 'How to Break Up' and then directly confronts the pros and cons (and sometimes necessities) of online dating services. The writing style is both informal and compelling, and Sam's pastor's heart (and the tire-treads on that heart) are evident throughout."

> **Rosaria Butterfield**, Author, *The Gospel Comes with a House Key*

"Sam Andreades offers **provocative and profoundly insightful advice** for men and women about dating. This book is sure to make its readers think and rethink how they go about seeking a spouse."

> **Dr. Joel R. Beeke**, President, Puritan Reformed Theological Seminary, Grand Rapids, Michigan

"Sam has done it again! He has taken his pioneering, countercultural work on gender in his last book, *enGendered*, and applied it here for the church to one of her most misunderstood topics: dating. The Church in America is between a rock and a hard place with regard to this topic. On the one hand, she struggles to disciple people in an overly sexualized culture which views relationships as disposable and transactional. On the other hand, the Church is still grappling with the damage of past teaching on dating that was unbiblical, reactionary, and legalistic. Between that Scylla and Charybdis, Sam offers this **refreshing and super-practical** book — from teaching on how to break up with someone to twelve questions for knowing if you are Mr. Right or if your date is Mr. Wrong. I will be mass-distributing it in my church!"

> **Geoff Bradford,** Senior Pastor of Christ the King Presbyterian Church, Raleigh, and Philadelphia church-planter

"As a Pastor, it breaks my heart to see, on the one hand, so many marriages fail and then, on the other, to see marriages never take place as people are finding it increasingly difficult to find a suitable spouse. Even though online dating promises an abundance of 'matches,' I hear story after story of how difficult it is to date successfully. I'm deeply thankful for Dr. Andreades, a reliable guide in assisting men and women to navigate the complexities of dating in our present cultural context. The author **skillfully avoids legalism while at the same time providing an abundance of practical help** that is deeply rooted in Scripture in general, and in a theology of gender in specific. I highly recommend this important book and would love to see the book have a massive impact."

> **Darin Pesnell**, Senior Lead Pastor of Iron Works Church, Phoenixville, and Head of the Iron Works Church Planting Network

Acknowledgments

To all the people herein to whom I have been pastor, or who have shared their story with me, please accept my gratitude for teaching me through your lives. Thank you to my family and the faithful people of Iron Works Church, without whose thoughtful critique this would be a much weaker book. I also offer many thanks to Tasha Chapman, Paul Brinkerhoff, Greg Perry and Marco Silva for their close reading and helpful comments on this book or *enGendered*.

CruciformPress

We publish clear, useful, biblically faithful, and mostly short books for Christians and other curious people. Books that tackle serious subjects in a readable style. We do this because the good news of Jesus Christ—the gospel—is the only thing that actually explains why this world is so wonderful and so awful all at the same time. Even better, the gospel applies to every single area of life, and offers real answers that aren't available from any other source.

Dating with Discernment: 12 Questions to Make a Lasting Marriage

Print / PDF ISBN: 978-1-949253-18-4
Mobipocket ISBN: 978-1-949253-19-1
ePub ISBN: 978-1-949253-20-7

Contents

PART I: Before You Leave the House

PART II: Is This the One?

~~~ INTERLUDE: Meet the Family! ~~~

PART III: Am I the One?

Part I
Before You Leave the House

Parts II and III of this book give you twelve questions to evaluate your dating relationship, to make the dangerous decision: *Is this one THE one that I should marry?* But before we leave the house for our first date, we need some principles to date well. Part I is about readying you for the romantic road. If you are anxious to get right to the questions, go on ahead to Part II. But if you want to review the dating process itself, let's first get a few things straight.

Chapter 1, "How to Break Up: Bearing Necessary Detours," advises on the first principle of dating: do not enter a dating relationship without a path to exit it. Breakups are a necessary aspect of dating, and you need to be able to do them gracefully. So it is worth assuring yourself with "the date who always shows up." This first relationship, which underlies all relationships, helps you consider your disengagement plan.

Chapter 2, "How to Get a Good Date: Guard the Gold," explains the second critical principle of dating: knowing the great treasure that God has created in you. This knowledge allows you to "guard the gold" of your body and soul. Only when you guard the gold can you enter the quest with a chance at success.

Chapter 3, "How to Date Wisely: An Enduring

Approach," surveys the trouble that marriage is in today and takes us on a trek to discover what to do about it as daters. The problem is not dating itself. Neglect of trustworthy advisors, suspect marriage-preparation methods, and our misconceptions about what happens in dating all contribute to the failure to make lasting unions. The Bible points the way forward for us: its counter-cultural counsel, highlighting gender in romantic relationships, supplies the approach to making marvelous marriages from the beginning.

You know, the Bible really is great. It seems magically put together to help us in every phase of life. It entertains us as children in Sunday School with its delightful stories, all the while pulling us toward goodness. As we grow, it puts up boundaries where we need them, and promises hope when we are despairing. When we become teenagers, the book of Ecclesiastes walks with us through existential crisis. When we marry, the Song of Solomon reassures us that our flaming passions are right and fitting. (As a young single man, I couldn't even read the Song of Solomon—it was a source of temptation to me. But when I got married, it sure became relevant.) I could go on and on, how the Psalms meet and guide our emotions, how the letters of Paul cultivate our intellect in the right directions, how Judges lets our sense of adventure soar, how we can have a psychedelic experience in the pages of Revelation, even without doing any drugs. And, of course, how through it all we are guided to salvation through the gospel of Jesus Christ.

It should not surprise us then that the Bible is also there for us as we date.

Chapter 4, "An Ancient Secret," explains this biblical approach. The questions of Parts II–III are based on the deep principles of intergendered relationship found in our origins. The first romantic comedy (of Adam and Eve) teaches us how men and women *together* display the image of God. Knowing why we date and why we get married gives us the wisdom and the confidence to ask the questions we should ask of our dates and ourselves.

So before you shiver at the sound of the doorbell, before you grit your teeth and make the phone call, even before you nervously hit *<Enter>* on the dating app profile, let's begin with the end.

One

How to Break Up: Bearing Necessary Detours

"The problem is all inside your head," she said to me
"The answer is easy if you take it logically
I'd like to help you in your struggle to be free
There must be fifty ways to leave your lover."
— Paul Simon[1]

My son, if you have put up security for your neighbor, have given your pledge for a stranger, if you are snared in the words of your mouth, caught in the words of your mouth, then do this, my son, and save yourself, for you have come into the hand of your neighbor: go, hasten, and plead urgently with your neighbor. Give your eyes no sleep and your eyelids no slumber; save yourself like a gazelle from the hand of the hunter, like a bird from the hand of the fowler.
— Solomon, son of David, king of Israel [a]

An Essential Angling Skill (Especially Online)

Come on! How to break up? What an awful way to start a book about successful dating. Can't I at least put this at the end—you know, where you might not have to read it?

Sorry, I cannot. I do not want to discourage you, but I have some disappointing news for you up front. The time may come when you need to say *goodbye* to the one

---

a. Pro 6:1–5.

you are dating. After all your hard work in joining, it may still end in a parting. As difficult as this is, you must be able to do it. If you are not able to end a dating relationship, you should never start one.

We all have the dream of finding Mr. or Mrs. "Right" right away, that the first crush will be the last, that the first doorbell ring will ring the final wedding bells. But that is often not the story the Lord gives us—and this is His mercy. Therefore, as you go in, you must be prepared to go out.

If you are using an online service to meet someone, this is especially pertinent. Dating apps and online services aren't wrong to use, but you need to go in with your eyes open to the features of the medium. Online dating services seem wonderful because they offer such a large pool of eligible candidates, so much larger than what you are finding in your boring old hometown or your cheerless church confines. But be prepared. Since you are starting without any context whatsoever, you will probably be breaking up more times before getting married. A relationship begun online is starting from scratch, with no life, no church, and no family background. Without the benefit of families living in community, or a church where we see personalities tested, you need to work harder to get to know the other person.

So, online dating actually makes the principles of this book more important. No online profiling asks you the questions that you will get here. Maybe they cannot. These questions can only really be answered by spending time doing things with one another in person.

***

"Deloris," a young woman in my congregation, came to me troubled about her boyfriend, "Russ." (Like all the names used in this book except for some of my own family, Deloris and Russ are pseudonyms. But their story is real.) They seemed supremely compatible—or at least so she thought. But they had been going together for several years with no movement forward. Deloris was a delightful person, the kind who never seemed to run out of energy. She was pretty. She had a strong grasp of the kind of theology on which one could set up a life. Her hands were always serving others. From what she told me, Russ had a lot of good qualities too. Deloris was so good at making other parts of her life work out. There was no reason this part should not be working also. Why wasn't it? Russ just wasn't asking.

This situation may sound like a cliché, but it doesn't feel like a cliché if you are living it. When we met, I did not have to say much to Deloris. She basically counseled herself in front of me. Russ was not going to close the deal. All these years had made the point; he just wasn't. It was time to "cut bait." Cutting bait is an angling expression of obscure origin that has come to mean giving up on the current effort in order to move on. In fishing terms, sometimes you can neither land the fish nor remove the hook. So you must cut the line and let you both go your separate ways (The freed fish usually extracts the hook on its own within a few days and goes on with his fish life.[2]) This was what Deloris needed to do. And she did. I was relieved. I told her that if there was a future with him, he'd be back. But it would have to be a different relationship with different parameters.

Of course, how long you have been seeing someone makes a big difference in how you feel about breaking up. If you have totaled two dates with the person, ending it is less painful than if you have been together for two years or — God forbid — ten. The latter breaking up feels harder than the sooner just breaking it off, but this chapter applies to both. Whether two weeks or two years, the way to get through the discomfort in a way that is bearable, even helpful, is to always have another lover in the wings.

The Date Who Always Shows Up

Before the day you say *I do,* you always have to be able to say, *I don't.* In your heart, you must be able to not date, even if you really want to. You may think, *Easy to say, but I am desperate.* You may feel, as Bruce Springsteen sung in his breakthrough album, standing in front of the porch screen door pleading to Mary, "Don't turn me home again; I just can't face myself alone again." God gives us different life aids to help in such a situation. Having a loving church and a supportive family are balms to your dread of loneliness. But the primary way you become able to lose a lover is by having Christ as your lover. He offers Himself to us as single people just this way.

Thus, this book in your hands turns out to be a book primarily useful for Christians. It is not just the emphasis on the Bible. I have found Christians to have great raw materials to make the dangerous decision well and embark on a wonderful marriage. If you, kind reader, are not a believer, you may well be offended at what I have to say in this book. (Come to think of it, even if you are a believer, you may well be offended at what I have to say.) But, of course, dear non-Christian, you are welcome to read and take any advice herein you find helpful. And perhaps, without a faith commitment to Jesus Christ, some of it can be useful for you. But you'll notice at certain points that the motivation and the goal of marriage for Christians is necessarily very Christ-oriented. Just saying.

At the Last Supper, Jesus is at His most tender with His disciples—and us.[a] The church has rightly interpreted these eleven apostles to stand for all of Jesus's followers as they receive the Lord's pledges of love, prayers for coherence, confirmations of comfort, and promises of power. In fact, Jesus even prays, "I do not ask for these only, but also for those who will believe in me through their word."[b] That would be us.

So it is particularly significant how Jesus opens this discourse to His church. He starts with what is best taken as the language of nuptial engagement.[3] In that first-century Jewish culture, a newly married couple would begin life together in an extension to the groom's father's house.[4] Unless the groom had his own house, his proposal meant going and building an addition onto the family home in which he and his new bride could live.[5] After this preparation of rooms, on the night of the wedding procession, the groom would return and take the bride to his father's house, their new home.[6] Earlier in this Gospel, John the Baptist evoked this picture of Jesus as the returning Jewish fiancé to get His bride.[c] Not long before this supper, Jesus

---

a. Joh 14–17.
b. Joh 17:20.
c. Joh 3:29.

also told stories about this cultural feature, identifying Himself as the departing and returning bridegroom.[a] [7]

This background makes sense of Jesus's imagery at the beginning of His speech. He says to them (and us):

> Do not let your hearts be troubled. Trust in God; trust also in me. In my Father's house are many rooms; if it were not so, I would have told you. I am going there to prepare a place for you. And if I go and prepare a place for you, I will come back and take you to be with me that you also may be where I am.[b]

Given what a bridegroom had to do to prepare a life for his intended, this is basically a marriage proposal, appropriate words to speak to one's bride-to-be during a betrothal. According to rabbinic law, the promises of the evening betrothal ceremony were serious business. The groom enumerated in detail what he was going to do for her.[8] Jesus said His words on the evening before He was going to pay the *mohar*, or bridal price, with His blood. Here, in this moment, the people of Christ become the bride of Christ.[c] In Jewish custom of that time, several years might separate the betrothal from the marriage as the groom prepared the rooms.[9] We are now living in that time of waiting before Christ's second coming, His return to get us for the "marriage" of heavenly union with Him.[d]

In the midst of this promise's beautiful imagery, we should not miss what Jesus is saying in His third sentence.

---

a. Mat 25:1–10.
b. Joh 14:1–3 (NIVO).
c. As imaged also in Mat 9:15; Mar 2:19–20; 2Co 11:2.
d. Rev 19:6–9.

He does not say, "If there weren't these rooms to be prepared for us, I wouldn't be telling you that there were." That kind of statement would make sense to say, and it would be honorable to say: "I am not making a false promise." But this proposer rather says something even more honorable. He says, "If it were *not* so, I *would have* told you." In other words, His intentions would have come out much sooner along the way. Jesus is telling them, and us, that He wouldn't have allowed us to think that we were really getting engaged with God Himself if there were no engagement coming. He would have taken care for our feelings. Simply put, He has not just been leading us on. This will not end in bitter tears of disappointment for us. That is why He tells them, "Do not let your hearts be troubled." Instead, let your hopes soar.

Especially if we are single, we should see in Jesus's words an invitation to live out our relationship with God in engagement terms. It may be uncomfortable to think about Jesus speaking this way to a group of guys in a closed room. But Jesus is ever one to be free with His metaphors.[10] Soon after, he takes to calling them orphans.[a] Just as God is a Father to orphans and a Husband to widows,[b] so also He is a Fiancé to single folks.[c] If you allow Him to be that, He is enough for you. If He is your ultimate date, you can date well. If He is not, you are liable to lack the inner strength to treat your dates as they need to be, or to be treated by them as you need to be.

If you crave love, there is no better place to find it,

---

a. Joh 14:18.
b. Deu 10:18; Psa 10:14; Psa 10:18; Psa 68:5; Psa 146:9; Jer 49:11; Hos 14:3.
c. Hos 2:19-20.

guy or girl—no gender distinction here. For man and woman in the bride of Christ, you find an answer to your loneliness in how He loves us. In fact, the reason you are currently single is to learn to receive this love of God. And if you do, you will be miles ahead in the dating game. Miles ahead in life, for that matter.

Cutting Bait for the Right Catch

You may not be able, for any number of reasons, to achieve a happy future with a particular someone. Differences in age, culture, education, or background present problems that can be overcome, but one shouldn't be naïve about the obstacles. Other more serious problems may bring you to a breakup. On several occasions I have had to advise daters to cut bait like Deloris did. Sometimes it was because the girl he was dating could not forgive and had no interest in learning how. Sometimes it was because the guy she was dating clearly would not take responsibility where he needed to. Sometimes one was just being strung along by the other. When too many of the answers to this book's questions come up as *no*, you need to be able to do it before it becomes a whole category of harder to let go. In these cases, having Christ as your first heartthrob will spare you an SUV of tears.

* * *

Joy was a young woman on the adventure of living in New York City. She had her head on basically straight, but she also had a thing for guitar players. It wasn't entirely rational. She liked the guitar herself, so she especially liked guys who played the guitar. And thus followed a string of relationships that weren't so great. While living in the city, she became a Christian. I remember when she came to the point of saying, "No more guitar players!" She made up her mind. She was through with dating that kind of guy. That was the old her.

Of course, I don't think that she meant to insult guitar players. For Joy, it was really a deeper decision of giving up her need to be with someone, anyone. Christ's love had filled her heart to the point that she was able to envision herself alone, rather than herself with someone who was wrong for her. Each person, man and woman, must reach a similar point to date well. Why is this so important first? Can't you just want Jesus and a date equally at the same time? And, you know, let God purify your motives as time goes on? Believe me, there will be plenty of God purifying your motives as time goes on, but you will save yourself a dishwasher full of despair by getting this right beforehand. You must be ready to not be married so you can have a good marriage.

Seven Steps to Doing a Good Breakup

So, when you need to, here is how you do it.

1. Break up with bravery. You may not be breaking up because of a lack of chemistry between you. Maybe there is great chemistry. But you have come to realize that chemistry is not what makes a marriage.[a] I have chemistry

---

a. Pro 31:30.

with a lot of women. But that doesn't mean that we could
co-build a home.

* * *

Carter sat in conversation with Charlene with a sober look
on his face. It was difficult, what he had to do, but he was
sure he had to do it. What made it all the more difficult
was that Carter had had two previous serious relationships
that didn't work out. He now looked back on them with
regret. As he told it to me, when they hit some conflict,
he was not mature enough then to know how to address
it. He felt that he let those women get away. Carter was
also in his thirties now and feeling a pang when he saw his
peers already in marriages with growing families.

Even more trying for the breakup were the great
things about this woman. I knew Char. She was a committed follower of Christ and a very beautiful girl. She
was clearly willing to move forward. She had wanted them
to talk about engagement at their three-month dating
mark. They had conducted their relationship with honor.
But now, seven months in, Carter ended their engagement, choosing to face the ways the relationship was not
working rather than just letting things move to marriage
by momentum.

I felt sad for them at the time. We all want our friends'
romances to work out. But I also remember admiring
Carter's courage in doing this, because I knew how he
wanted to be married. Sometimes our friends' romances
shouldn't work out. This was one of those times.

2. Talk in person. This might seem obvious now, away
from the roar of battle, but never underestimate how

cowardly we can be. You do not break up with someone
by phone, email or — God forbid — text.

* * *

Hakeem sat in the back seat of the Humvee, on maneu-
vers out in the woods of Michigan, staring at his phone.
He was feeling more alone than ever as he read the words
over and over. The text just said, "I don't think this will
work out." And that was it. She was breaking things off.
He couldn't respond. He couldn't talk to the guys he was
with, as he didn't know them well. He couldn't contribute
to her decision or learn from it. That was just it.

As with all situations in life, Jesus calls you to treat
a person as you wish you would be treated if the situation were reversed.[a] How can you show your soon to be
ex-boyfriend or ex-girlfriend respect that is due them as
image-bearers of God?[b] Have the painful meeting, if at
all possible, face to face. If you are so long-distance that
this is impractical, still do it in some way that shows the
person that he or she is important.

3. Honor the other with gratitude. Unless you just
found out that she was stealing from you, or that he was
deliberately using you to get a job with your father (or
something more awful), there are probably many things
you can list that you appreciate about the other person.
After all, you wanted to date, didn't you? These are good
for that person to hear. I went through several breakups —
initiating, receiving, and mutual — before I dated the woman
I married. Some of them were not pretty. But by the time of

a. Luk 6:31.
b. Gen 5:1-2.

the last ended romance, I had made this the centerpiece of a parting of ways. It made a big difference. Again, wouldn't you want to hear about your strengths as well as your weaknesses to be able to move forward with hope?

4. Be direct. Yes, you should be honest about the "why."[a] You can certainly speak in humility, acknowledging that this is only your view, that you are limited in how you see things, and that you could be wrong. But *it is* your view. Whatever you do, do not drop out of contact without explanation (aka ghosting). If you have been ghosted, you know how wrong it feels. Don't leave this step of directness out because all breakups are actually a step of discipleship. Though difficult, you can both walk away from this experience having grown a good deal wiser about yourselves. You are doing both of you an important service. Whether you are on the initiating side, the receiving side, or it is mutual, let it happen.

5. Deliver a vision of hope. My wife, no stranger to breakups (not with me, fortunately), wisely advises including a vision of a brighter future for the other person. It is not insincere to express hope for his life, or to describe your faith in God about her, if you really do believe that there is a better plan for both your lives.

The Bible's story of Paul and Barnabas is not about a romantic relationship, but it shows the same principle at work. At one point, the apostle Paul and Barnabas break up their close church-planting partnership.[b] Their disagreement is so sharp, they had to part ways. But their

---

a. Pro 27:6.
b. Acts 15:36–40.

resolution, of divvying up the churches they planted and visiting them separately,[a] expresses hope for each other in the service of their Lord. Five or six years later, Barnabas comes up in one of Paul's letters.[11] It is clear from how Paul lumps Barnabas and himself together that Paul considered the man a "partner" in the work.[b] Paul thereby expresses hope for his brother even though they no longer worked together. Spend some time living in that dream of hope for the other person before the conversation.

* * *

Stella and Austin dated for a couple months, but it was not going to work. She was country and he was rock-and-roll. He planned restaurant dates while she wanted to walk through a field without their shoes on. So they broke up. A few months afterward, when Austin checked on how she was doing, Stella mentioned a friend whom she thought might really enjoy meeting him. It was a nice thought, but Austin was shocked when Stella walked into the club on 13th Street where he was DJ'ing with said friend, Nova, in tow. From there, the sparks just flew. Today Austin and Nova are happily married, living with three children on an urban street. Stella herself has her own growing family. They go camping a lot. I have heard more than one story like this of how an ex-boyfriend's or ex-girlfriend's introduction worked out. Sometimes the feelings are difficult after a friend you introduced does indeed start dating your ex, but you have done a great deed in delivering a vision of hope for the other person.

---

a. Acts 15:39–40.
b. 1Co 9:6.

6. *End it with definiteness.* The disentangling imagery
of Proverbs 6:1–5 that opened this chapter describes
breakup situations well: Flee like a gazelle. Escape like
a bird from the hand of the fowler. Purpose not to be in
contact with this "neighbor" in any way for X number of
months. The ease of the familiar can be your enemy here.
A breakup is a breakup. Even if some changes occur that
later might revive the possibility of reuniting, you should
not entertain that thought now. Do not continue engaging
with the other's social media content (digital orbiting) or
allow popping up again after a time without notice (sub-
marining). Delete the contact information.

The one-time couple above, Austin and Stella, made
a wise rule of six months without contact. It truly helped
clean the slate. If one of you wants to "just stay friends,"
you should be extra clear about limiting contact. The most
merciful incision is made with a sharp knife.

7. Take time to heal. Maybe this breakup is not a big
deal to you, or maybe you are devastated. But at the very
least, it is a disappointment. Scripture nails the description of this situation with the words, "Hope deferred
makes the heart sick."[a] So your sick heart needs some
time to heal. Give yourself that time to feel the pain of this
deferred hope. Let your heart grieve.

These steps don't cover all of your individual circumstances, but at least get these right. Then return to the arms
of your Savior, your promised bridegroom, and let Him
be your portion.[b] And recognize that the best decisions of

---

a. Pro 13:12.
b. Lam 3:24.

our lives are usually the most painful. They make a way for great things in the future.

The story of you is not over. It wasn't over for Joy. Remember her back in New York, swearing off guitar players? Soon after making that resolution, Joy met Bruno, an entirely different class of guy. She found out how, very often, breakup events become a doorway to a much better match. These two have now been happily wed for many years. And, by the way, Bruno, the husband that has made Joy so happy, is also a very good guitar player.

Two

How to Get a Good Date: Guard the Gold

Han Solo: Look, Your Worshipfulness, let's get one thing straight. I take orders from just one person: me
Princess Leia Organa: It's a wonder you're still alive.
— George Lucas [12]

'Tis safest in matrimony to begin with a little aversion.
— Richard Brinsley Sheridan [13]

An Impossible Dream

Albert was shy. He developed a crush on Allyson, who had him seeing hearts in the clouds. But he didn't know if she could imagine him up there in the clouds with her. Mrs. D, as she was known, was a tour-de-force of a language teacher. He didn't know how it came up, but Albert found himself talking to Mrs. D about this girl. When he shared his affections for Allyson with Mrs. D, her response was forceful. She cut to the quick: "Do you like her? You gotta ask her out!" Mrs. D insisted. "You have to do it now." Well, Mrs. D's confidence spilled off onto Albert. *Yeah!*, he thought, *Maybe Allyson is just waiting to say yes to me.* Not knowing what awaited him, he asked her. And he was rejected. Allyson actually appeared afraid of him. Albert tried to salvage the conversation. "Can I just call you?" he asked, pitifully. "Okay," she said, "but just as a friend." He was devastated.

When the news got back to Mrs. D, her attitude shocked Albert. "Oh well," she said. "Time to move on to another one." *Another one? What other one could there be?* But the judgment had been made. The gavel had landed. Allyson had delivered the decision of the universe: Albert was a reject.

This is a very funny story to me because, just a few years later, Albert was being chased—almost literally—by a number of women. I wish I could show you the pictures of the women who would have given anything to belong to him. What changed? Nothing, really. It was just a different setting, different people, different circumstances. Albert ended up with none of these willing maidens. He surprised his friends with another woman entirely, and today he has a large happy family with her.

The girls at first did not recognize Albert's value. So he didn't either. But it is not just Albert. When I started to try to date, I found myself obsessing over different women at different times. Four of them, when I asked, turned me down flat: Madilyne, Lynda, Robyn, and then Blanche. I got an absolute no. There wasn't even a pause in their voices. These crushes turned out to be crushing. As single people, we all doubt whether someone could actually love us. It drives a lot of what we do. My parents may love me, and that helps, but they kind of have to. My friends may like to hang around me, but that is just being friends. If I am popular or garner a large online following or accumulate a captive audience, I can get mass affection.

They may even clap. But those people do not really know me. And if they did, could they actually love me? *Me*?

The Marty Syndrome

I do not know how confident you are as a person. But I do know that you carry around inside you an underlying shame. It's been there ever since... well, way back, when the human race made a decision to close its heart to the greatest love of all. More precisely, Adam, someone who perfectly and accurately represented you, made that decision,[a] and you and I followed suit.[b] Ever since then, we have doubted if we could be loved.[c] And the single life accentuates this doubt: the doubt that somebody worth something could see me and want me. This is why some single people do not want to date, and do not even want to try to meet someone. Dating spotlights the question: *Could I actually be loved?* For some who really doubt themselves, it is easier to not even raise the question. Deep down, they think that they already know the answer.

I call this the Marty Syndrome. I derive the term from a 1955 movie called *Marty*,[14] written by Paddy Chayefsky. The way dating highlights this self-doubt has never been better captured than in this utterly natural story of an unmarried Brooklyn butcher. Well-meaning neighborhood matriarchs keep asking him when he is going to marry. Guy friends keep telling him tempting stories of seducing women and promoting porn to him. (It is the

---

a. Gen 3:6.
b. Rom 5:12; 1Co 15:22.
c. Gen 3:7-10.

1950s, so it is soft porn, but it is the same thing.) Dances put on to help single people meet each other feel like beauty contests. These scenes display the worst parts of dating. The undue importance of what your friends think. The awkward first moments and missteps of a relationship. The insecurity. The rejection. The butcher (played wonderfully by Ernest Borgnine), alternates between trying to address his loneliness by going out to meet people, and just being fed up with the whole business.

The picture won Best Screenplay, Best Director, Best Actor and Best Movie for that year. It is one of only two American films ever to win both the Cannes Film Festival and the Palme d'Or international prizes. Why the success on such a mundane topic? Because it discloses something about ourselves we all know is true. Our sin-shame makes it hard to imagine that we are valuable enough to love. It is worth watching if you are starting to date, as it also affords a comparative peek into dating customs of the American 1950s. Even without seeing the movie, though, if you are a single person who is getting older, you know just what I am talking about.

Our condition of shame also accounts for the intoxication of falling in love. Do you wonder why lovers can be so smitten? Why do their sandwiches sit on their plates half-eaten? Why do they neglect their cherished friends and long-held hobbies? Why do they forget to feed the cat? They cannot concentrate on their work anymore. They are not much good for parties. They even abandon you on the basketball court, one shy of a playable game. Why? Because that doubt about whether anyone of value could love them is, for a moment, dispelled. Nothing compares to that feeling. Other sensations pale. It is a form of being drunk.

I wish this experience for you. I cannot guarantee it, but I can guarantee something else. The answer to the haunting question is *yes*: You are worthy of love. You are worth being wanted. I know that this is true about you. I can tell, even though I haven't met you, because the Father created you. Because the Holy Spirit is testifying it to you repeatedly. And because, if you can receive it, Jesus Christ went to the cross for you.

The Treasure You Are

How do you know if a girl really likes you? There is what your friends say, or her friends say, but there could be other things going on there. Really, how do you know that a guy really does want you? There are myriad women's magazine articles giving you the signs: certain phrases he uses or a glimmer in how he looks at you. But then some of those might turn out to be a guy's indigestion. Really, how do you know if you are, in fact, loved? It is when he gets jealous. It is when her skin turns a tad greenish with envy over your involvement with other women or pursuits.

* * *

Rebekah walked around for a few days stewing. She realized that she was angry with Troy, her long-distance boyfriend. They had been dating for several months. But Troy posted a picture of himself with a friend, a girl, on

Instagram. He commented on the post about the good time they were having hanging out. Troy had known this other friend a long time, and there was nothing untoward going on, but Rebekah was bothered by Troy's post. It led to an argument, making it abundantly clear that Troy had her heart.

Certainly, there is a bad kind of controlling jealousy, but God says, rather bluntly, that jealousy is part of who He is. He calls Himself a jealous God[a] and flat-out advertises that *His name is Jealous.*[b] God's jealousy for His people comes out of a commitment to them called a covenant.[c] Jesus poetically referenced that commitment, as we saw in the previous chapter, when He "proposed" to His followers. If you belong to the Lord, this "very flame of the Lord"[d] burns for you and what is best for you.

Like Rebekah to Troy, God shows you this jealousy in the gospel of Jesus Christ to convince you of the treasure you are. Christ's sacrifice for you is God's jealous flame. When a holy God feels that way about you, it dispels the doubt of your lovability. You get a sense of the holiness of your person, to which no one should have easy access. When you know God's treasuring, you are ready to date in a way that guards the gold. If you don't, dating can do you deep damage.

---

a. Deu 6:15.
b. Exo 34:14.
c. Exo 34:10.
d. Sos 8:6.

How to Do Yourself Deep Damage

Ellie, a girl I was once dating, mentioned to me nonchalantly, "I'd definitely want to live with someone first before we got married. Otherwise how could I tell if I was compatible with him?" I know what Ellie was thinking. Trying out that part of marriage with someone before making a commitment seems to make sense because marriage is such a big deal. Why not experiment by living together first? Why not avoid harming people by a marriage plus a divorce? Still, I thought, does Ellie not realize the pain coming her way? We broke up soon afterward. We were just heading in very different directions.

Sex outside of marriage, what used to be called fornication, is now called hooking up and cohabitation. Living and sleeping together outside a marital covenant is a way of not guarding the gold. It deeply damages both parties. So social statistics consistently say, and so they are just as consistently ignored. Back in the 1990s, studies clearly showed the failure of cohabitation to prepare for marriage, or even achieve personal satisfaction.[15] Even so, cohabitation in America doubled from 1990 to 2008, rising then to over six million households.[16] By 2010, it was well-known that cohabitation is not only less stable than marriage, it is less stable than *re-marriage* (marrying another after a divorce). Only 13 percent of cohabitations remain intact after five years, compared with 77 percent of re-marriages.[17] And a recent assessment in *Psychology Today* highlighted research showing that people with more sexual encounters or more experience living with

a partner are measurably less likely to have quality marriages later on.[18] Cohabitating couples are more likely, on
average, to experience infidelity and domestic violence
than married couples.[19] Children in a cohabiting household are more likely to have run-ins with the law, fail in
school, do drugs, and experience depression. Even more
disturbing, "children in cohabiting step-families are 98
percent more likely to be physically abused, 130 percent
more likely to be sexually abused, and 64 percent more
likely to be emotionally abused, compared with children
in married step-families."[20] In short, this defective practice
leaves ravaged human souls along a trail of tears.

Why is this so? Sex is a great thing,[a] even a holy thing,[b]
and so can be greatly misused.[c] When we take sex out of
marriage, we misuse it. The prophet Jeremiah was a brass-
tacks kind of guy. He once remarked, "You go after other
gods to your own harm."[d] Jeremiah was saying that when
people follow other gods, not doing life as the true God
says to, it damages them. Sinning—that is, disregarding
how God tells us to live—not only offends God, which
is bad enough; it also wrecks our lives.[e] The apostle Paul
explains that kind of self-harm when saying that the forni-
cator not only sins against another but also dishonors his
own body.[f] That is why it awakens God's jealousy and He
forbids it. These prophets warn against this abuse of the
gift of sex because of the ruin it brings to us, to which the
statistics and the Scriptures testify.

---

a. Pro 30:18–19.
b. 1Co 7:1–5; Heb 13:4.
c. Pro 30:20.
d. Jer 7:6.
e. Deu 10:13.
f. 1Th 4:3–6.

When the Past Comes Back

Treyvon could not hide his dismay from Zahra. After many years, God had finally restored him to godly manhood. And after so many failed relationships, he considered it the Lord's great mercy to have such a wonderful, devout, beautiful wife in Zahra. They had been married for over a year, but each time they made love, Treyvon told me, he was plagued with regret. His experience with multiple partners came back to him at just the wrong times, times he should only be sharing with Zahra. He deeply desired sex to be solely about Zahra now, but certain memories intruded into their relationship. I told him that better days were ahead, but I could not downplay the power of the past to invade one's bedroom in the present.

Sex is like Crazy Glue. It seems from the way it gets marketed like it should be neat and tidy to use. But every time you open the tube, you are liable to glue your fingers together. Getting them apart will not occur without skin loss. With sex, if you attach yourself to someone and then tear away, you leave a piece of yourself behind. Some of you is torn from you, and you enter the next relationship a little more ripped up and lacking. Yes, that is a graphic picture, but that is what is happening if you buy in to cohabitation. Again, Paul portrays multiple sexual experiences outside of marriage as a sin against your own body.[a] Until you become cynical about it, you can tell that physical intimacy bonds you together like a powerful epoxy. People going through this the first time know it. After the second or third person, they just stop caring about it.

---

a. 1Co 6:15–18.

Even more tragic is the entire secular generation now being raised on hookup culture, which is kind of like anti-dating. The Christian church is not unaffected: most of those who identify as Christians and use dating websites are quite willing to have casual sex.[21] Based on a debased view of sex as an evolutionary vestige of the need to propagate the species, hooking up is a quick road to self-destruction, even for the guys for whom casual hookups are supposed to be the great fantasy.[22] The hookup culture exacerbates the trauma of single-ness because it forces detachment. Instead of sex being a process of becoming vulnerable, it becomes the opposite: a process of distancing. During the hookup you must encrust your heart to protect it. It is a sickening parody of what lovemaking was meant to be. It teaches both of you how to lose hope that there is committed love. As the hookup generation grows up into polyamory, even more hopelessness will settle in. These cultural devolutions are throwing the gold overboard.

But this multiplying of sorrows does not have to be yours. Even if this is your past, it does not have to be your future. Instead, according to God, you are a treasure chest containing gold. Man or woman, there are things about you that He especially created for another's enjoyment. God takes delight in your gold Himself. Then, perhaps, He gives another to delight in your gold, someone He gives to remind you of Him. You cannot date well without knowing this. And when you do know this, you can form standards and brave the dating game.

Lining Up at the Starting Blocks

The opening Chapter of the book of Judges makes an important point about finding a marriage partner. To see that, we need to understand the point of the book. Judges shows us the downward spiral of society when godly, committed leadership is lacking in a nation. Because "in those days there was no king in Israel,"[a] an initially victorious society goes steadily downhill. A lot of this devolution has to do with the women as well as the men, and the relationship between them. This means that the best guys, the best gals, and the best situations are found at the beginning of the book, when times are good. So, when we read about marriage-making occurring in Chapter one, we are seeing dating in an ideal time. And what we see there is mate-finding as something of a competition.

First, there is Achsah. In a righteous move her father, Caleb, sets up a quest to discover the best guy out there for her. It is just like the old fairy tales, only this happened in real life. The campaign to take the Promised Land has come to a halt because the city of Kiriath Sepher seems impossible to take. Caleb makes it known that the man who could lead a successful siege against that city would be the man for his daughter.[b] It is a sword-in-the-stone maneuver to find the man with great leadership gifting for his daughter—and it succeeds. The eventual winner, Othniel,[c] goes on to become the first[d] and most powerful commander of Israel's era of judges, a faithful leader of the

---

a. Jdg 17:6; Jdg 18:1; Jdg 19:1; Jdg 21:25.
b. Jdg 1:9–12.
c. Jdg 1:13.
d. Jdg 3:8–11.

people and an empire-defeater.[23] What is Caleb doing? He is helping his daughter to guard the gold.

Meanwhile, Othniel himself also welcomes this approach to mate-finding as a quest for the best girl for him. Apparently, she is quite a motivating prize. He responds to a problem requiring uncommon leadership. He goes out there, seeking the best girl that covenant, faithful leadership could win. He also is guarding the gold.

So it is not wrong to view dating as a quest for a prize. But it is a quest with many winners and no one grand prize. Thankfully, your heart is not a lock to which only one soul out there has the key. Rather, in cooperation with God's providence, you are looking for one worth enjoying your gold. Because finding a mate also depends upon God's gracious providence, I cannot guarantee that you will win a spouse. But if you play this game well, as we explore in chapter 11, you will not lose out on a prize.

The Various Glitters of Gold

Some men and women tend to shy away from the idea of finding a spouse as a competition. One big reason is that they fear that they will fail at it. Perhaps you do not feel like you can measure up in such a game. You feel you have a lengthy list of drawbacks. You have been at it too long. You were never confident at flirting. You do not come up with witty things to say.

Or perhaps you are not so great looking. Youth has a way of making almost all of us somewhat attractive, but let's say that looks are not your strong suit. You need to know something: good looks are great, but they are over-rated.[a] The degrading split-decision apps that invite us to swipe right to judge hot or not, to smash or pass, completely miss this. Beauty is certainly a good gift, and a powerful one for winning a mate,[b] but it is not the only one.[c] Go read the play *Cyrano de Bergerac,* or at least watch a movie like *Shrek* or *Shallow Hal,* to help yourself believe that this could be true. It is. God has distributed gifts amply to the people He makes.

The book of Proverbs was the training manual for the royal youth of the ancient Davidic Kingdom. The very section of Proverbs advising these Israelite young men of the royal court on women qualifies the ideal of beauty. The final passage of the book advises the youth on how to evaluate a woman for marriage, and its concluding two verses invite taking inventory of a feminine prospect. The author candidly acknowledges different qualities you could rank, such as beauty and charm.[d] But how a woman relates to the Lord comes out on top. In the long run this makes the greatest difference in the quality of a man's life and even, truth be told, in how good their sex is.

Eleanor was lounging across a chair in the fellowship hall after church. She had just finished nursing and was relaxing while listening to the trials of Harper, a younger single woman. Harper was bemoaning how guys are so fixated on a woman's appearance. It put so much pressure on her. Eleanor startled the young woman with her

---

a. Pro 11:22.
b. Gen 29:17–18.
c. 1Pe 3:4.
d. Pro 31:30.

counsel: "Your uptightness is working against getting a guy," she explained. "Look, I am sexier than you are." Now, just to note, having a baby often changes a woman's form. The demands of birthing and breastfeeding leave the body with a different shape. Eleanor had had a few babies already and had become somewhat chunky. Harper, on the other hand, had a noticeably youthful figure. But despite their relative bodies, Eleanor was right. Her confidence as a woman, her assurance of her gifts, did give her a superior sexuality, if I can put it that way. It is not all about looks.

You likely underestimate the attractions of your strengths. The trick to getting a good date is to find your best gifts and to flaunt them. What has the Lord given you to win a high-quality prize? You might be rejected by the first one you want. But that is not the end of the game.

One of the most romantic stories you may ever hear confronts us early on in the Bible, in the tale of a famous couple coming together. Their names were Boaz and Ruth. Ruth, a recent immigrant, was known to Boaz. She and her mother-in-law had come into hard times, and he had been kind to them. Ruth then came and rather forwardly offered herself to this man asleep on the threshing floor.[a] The euphemism used by the author, that she "uncovered his feet,"[b] is tricky to interpret. It could mean something much more than the feet. At the very least, it was a forward action. Boaz awakens and responds by blessing her: "May you be blessed by the LORD, my daughter. You have made this last kindness greater than the first in that

a. Rut 3:7–15.
b. Rut 3:7.

you have not gone after young men, whether poor or rich."[a]

This action and response tell us a few things. First, it tells us that Boaz was likely not that handsome. If he was, he wouldn't be commending Ruth for offering herself to him rather than some young handsome man. Second, it tells us that Ruth was probably very beautiful. Even after marrying and becoming a widow and lacking money and status, Boaz's words mean that she *could have* won another dashing, handsome or rich guy for herself. Third, it tells us that there was something else about Boaz, besides his looks, that won the beautiful Ruth. The rest of the book of Ruth tells us what it was: Boaz's covenant faithfulness and kindness to her mother-in-law and to her. If you haven't, you might want to read it.

Whatever you've got, I am going to teach you how to win this quest's prize. The task is not to find the only one person that you should be with. From our earthly perspective, we cannot know such a thing, and the Scriptures do not teach us to think that way. Rather, the quest before you is to win the best mate for you that you can. But you cannot even get out of the gate unless you are ready to enter the arena while guarding the gold.

Proverbs puts it this way: "He who finds a wife finds a good thing."[b] So let's go look.

---

a. Rut 3:10.
b. Pro 18:22.

Three

How to Date Wisely: An Enduring Approach

*And may the good gods give you all your heart desires:
husband, and house, and lasting harmony too. No finer,
greater gift in the world is that when man and woman
possess their home, two minds, two hearts that work as one.
It is despair to their enemies, a joy to all their friends, their
own best claim to glory.*
— Homer[24]

*Most choose their mate by moonlight, but a good farmer
wouldn't even choose a hog that way.*
— A hog farmer

The Princess of the South and the Princess of the North

Jake and Alan were best friends in college. One day, they discovered they shared something deep. Each had a growing conviction that he belonged with his high school girlfriend. Jake, growing up in the South, went out with Jill. Alan, from the Northeast, dated Amber. Although Jake and Alan had broken up with these girls years before, they couldn't get them out of their minds. They each set out to reconnect with these women, whom they privately called "the Princess of the South" and the "Princess of the North."

I should note that this is not uncommon in young men coming of age: the feeling that they should be with the girl that they were first with in high school. This comes of an original conviction in most men, unspoken and often unrecognized, that their first love should be their only love. This desire to be with one woman, and only one woman, is there in men in the beginning, before it is slapped around by rejection or betrayal, trampled down by lust, and eventually ground to dust by covetousness and cynicism. Sure enough, Alan and Jake each felt this primal conviction and embarked on a quest back to the headwaters, like leaping salmon. Both found the women receptive and began dating them again.

From there, their stories sadly diverged. Jake appeared to have great success with Jill. She was attracted to him as a handsome, Ivy League grad. Though they had some differences, these did not deter Jake. They talked about many marriage issues and got counsel from a few different sources on their points of tension. They married on a beautiful day in the early 1980s. Within a few years it turned rocky. I got involved at that point and offered some help, which restored things for a while. But ten years later they were divorced. Harmful repercussions plagued each of them and their children for decades.

Meanwhile Alan got together with Amber for a time. He had a way of dating that brought things to the surface early on. They soon realized that, as much as they shared and as much as they were attracted to one another, it was not going to work. They split up before getting too involved. Alan is now very happily married to another woman with whom he has raised a strong family. Amber was also doing well in her own marriage, the last I heard.

Neither high school flame, the Princess of the South nor the Princess of the North, was the right choice for these boys. What made the difference between their love stories?

Friends, We've Got Trouble

I don't want to propagate couplings that don't last. I want those who wish to marry to enjoy its sumptuous gifts, to drink in the intimacy and radiate the fruitfulness of a life-long, committed union of living, working, waking, and sleeping together. I want to help people thrive in marriage.

I don't have to tell you that people now have a lot of trouble doing this. The U.S. Census Bureau reports that since 2010, married couples make up less than half of all households (as shown in Figure 1). Let that sink in. Less than half.

People are finding it more difficult to marry, so the time it takes to get married is also getting longer and longer. The average age in America of first marriage is now 29.8 for men and 27.8 for women, according to this same U.S. Census Bureau. About fifty years ago, that average age was in the early twenties (Figure 2).

And for those who do marry, plenty now end in divorce. You can tell this simply by the cultural acceptance of divorce. People have become so accustomed to divorce that they are tentative in asking about the family of an acquaintance not seen for a while. It is safer to limit the

Figure 1

Percent of households by type

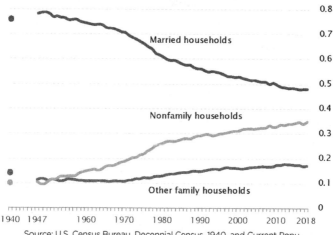

Source: U.S. Census Bureau, Decennial Census, 1940, and Current Population Survey, Annual Social and Economic Supplements, 1947 to 2018.

Figure 2

Median age at first marriage: 1890 to present

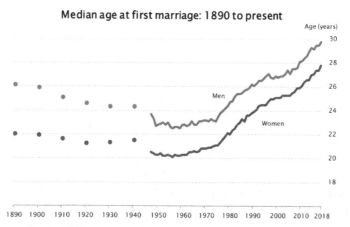

Source: U.S. Census Bureau, Decennial Census, 1890 to 1940, and Current Population Survey, Annual Social and Economic Supplements, 1947 to 1918

conversation to asking about the children. Some writers
these days speak optimistically about the rate of divorce
going down since 1980. This is true, but it is only because
there was such a spike in divorces in the 1970s. The recent
decline just masks the longer-term trend. The graph in
Figure 3 goes back to the year 1860. Just consider the frac-
tion of marriages that ended in divorce in the nineteenth
century compared to today. Undeniably, the United States
sees fewer marriages and more divorces.

I want to help you buck this trend. Because successful marriages are better than a billion dollars, better than
a garden full of gardenias, better than sliced bread, better
than most of the terrific things you could name. There is

Figure 3

Marriages and Divorces per Thousand People, United States 1860–2005

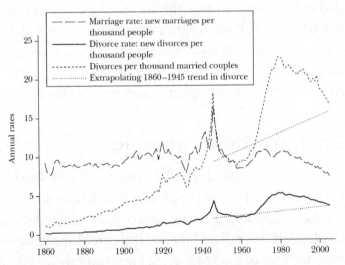

Betsey Stevenson and Justin Wolfers, "Marriage and Divorce: Changes and
Their Driving Forces," *Journal of Economic Perspectives* 21, no. 2 (2007): 29.

nothing in this world like marriage for anchoring your
soul in bliss and bringing blessing in life for yourself and
others. Physical health benefits. Wealth benefits. The
love that overflows in marriage becomes children for
the world and stability for your extended family. The
steady machinery of marriage makes better people of its
participants. The fruitfulness of marriage cannot help but
generate numerous exports of goodness: hospitality for
those in its orbit, financial prosperity for families around
it, the grounding of offspring by its love. Good marriage is
virtually the meaning of a sound culture, nothing less than
the bulwark of any society, in any place on earth, in any
time in history.

But more than all of that, there is nothing in the
world like marriage for showing us God. The Almighty
has a different plan for some; not all marry. But those who
do have a chance to reveal the image of God in a distinctive way. As we'll see, that fact gives us the secret to dating
well. So, yes, getting into a marriage that prospers might
be hard work, but it is worth working hard to get into.
And you can. Your prosperity can contradict the statistics.

Back to the Beginning

George sighed as we assessed the damage. He explained to
me his great realization concerning he and his wife's recent
breakup after more than ten years of marriage (and several
children). It dawned on him that their problems stemmed
from the time of their first dates. He could hardly believe
it, he explained, but as he looked all the way back, he saw
it. It was not only that the seeds of their current fights

could be seen in their communications at the beginning;
it was that the very pattern of their unhealthy interactions
began in their dates. I knew George and Frances then
too, before their marriage, and remembered how happy
they seemed to be. As a friend in the same church who
attended their wedding and threw rice at them, I had
not seen it coming. George was a great person. And so
was Frances. They were both quite smart and had done
thorough personality testing. George was now humbly
confiding in me, and I wept with him, but there was not
much I could do. They got divorced a few years later, with
many far-reaching consequences for their children and
themselves.

To help you marry well, we need to go back to the
beginning of a relationship and start there, at the early
decisions that two people make as they are dating. I first
developed this counsel for my own children. Two of them
have already gotten married and now I have two wonderful daughters-in-law. I also have a daughter and a son who
are now just dipping into the dating waters. My "children"
have also come to include the single folks in churches I've
pastored who desire marriage.

I say, "who desire marriage," because not everyone
gets married. Some single folks stay single. And this can
be a marvelous life. But staying single isn't what this book
is about. It's about getting married. In scriptural shorthand, this book is more Ephesians 5 than 1 Corinthians 7.
(If you do not know what I mean by that, go to the Bible
and compare those two Chapters).

The Roads Leading to Rome

So what is the best way to get into a good marriage?
And why are there so many bad ones? Maybe dating is
the problem. In some circles, Christians debate whether
dating is even a good thing to do. Who thought up dating
in the first place? Who said that this cultural convention,
the currently predominant way of the West, is the best
manner to mate? You might be one of those readers who
need first of all to see the practice itself justified. But let me
ask you, if you are not married and want to be, what are
the alternatives to dating? There are a few other choices,
I suppose. If we take a step back, we can espy several
different ways people have woken up to that glorious
morning when they look across the bed and find themselves married.

There are parent-arranged marriages, prevalent
throughout history and still how the majority of the
world gets married. They are generally backed by lower
divorce rates.[25] However abhorrent to Western sensibilities (such a practice offends our fierce independence),
we should grant that there are some advantages to this
method if wise caretakers are motivated out of love for
their children. Oak-solid parents, after all, ought to know
much better than these inexperienced saplings what will
make for a good marriage—that is, assuming that they
have one themselves. But downplaying or eliminating the
choice of the ones getting married seems to me to lose
something of the Bible's marriage mandate. In Genesis
2:24, God (or Adam, depending on who you think is
speaking at that point) defines marriage as a leaving of

father and mother: "Therefore a man shall leave his father
and his mother and hold fast to his wife, and they shall
become one flesh."

That "leaving," I have found, carries a lot of weight
for good marriages. It is the single person, not the parent,
who is doing the leaving, which is an act of his will. That
will of the man, and the woman also leaving her parents,
should be part of the process. Marriages that are strictly a
decision of the parents miss this. But parents who recognize this right of choice for their child can be invaluable in
the adventure.

There is using a matchmaker. Whether you are aware
of it or not, some people do this. It is part of a why-not-
leave-it-to-a-professional mindset. As a way to kick things
off, it is fine. But again, I cannot see bypassing the lovers'
decision or taking too much out of an individual's hands.

Similarly, there is using an online service, which is
increasingly the norm. Match Group, which operates the
most successful online dating websites (e.g., Match, Tinder,
PlentyOfFish), pulled in $1.7 billion in revenue in 2018.[26]
Do they work? Well, screens can only get things started.
They can help if you do not put too much weight on
what the algorithm spits out. But you want to get past the
screens as soon as possible.

Then there is courtship, which may be suited to
very young daters but may not fit most people's circumstances. If courtship just means something more like
purpose-driven dating, then okay, that is closer to what
healthy dating is anyway. Even if you are not explicit
about it or there is no defined time frame, a relationship

should be moving toward a goal. The kernel of goodness in courtship is directedness. At the back of any sincere dater's mind is always the question: *Is this "the one" I can spend the rest of my life with?* And if it isn't in your date's mind, that is not someone that you want to date. You will be used.

Hookups do not lead to marriage but actually make marriage harder to enter into. As the statistics of the previous chapter show, with each additional encounter of joining your bodies apart from knowing each other or committing to each other, you become less and less able to believe that love is real. Thankfully, Christ's salvation redeems us from all sin,[a] so there is a way back from even this wayward path, once we recognize it as such.

The long and short of it is: dating is what we have in the West. As cultural conventions go, it is not that bad. In fact, given the opportunities dating gives for really answering the questions needed to leave one's parents and make the dangerous decision, I think we should go with it. Maybe there is some better way, but this is what we've got. And from what I have seen, if properly used, chaste dating can work wonderfully.

Experienced Advisors Wanted

Even if we adopt dating as our method, in the face of the long-term marriage-meltdown trends, it is clear that we still need help with it. How do we get that aid? I shudder every time I look at the horrendous dating advice given

---

a. 1Co 6:9–11.

over the internet, often by well-degreed "relationship experts." Let's start closer to home. A prime place for you to get invaluable advice on dating is from your parents and your pastor. These advisors might get overlooked. But, if your relationship with them permits, you have an experienced voice close at hand. It is best if you can bring in a parent early on.

Frank credits his father with the crucial advice needed when he first started going out for coffee with Evelyn. Frank was a new believer and didn't know much. His dad took him aside to point out, for example, that if he intended get-togethers over coffee as dates, he needed to say so to Evelyn. It was a simple consideration, but one that young men today often miss. Frank did exactly that, along with taking other advice from his dad on the way to matrimony. Today, Frank and Evelyn are joyfully joined. They just had their second child.

God gives parents to be a weighty place of influence in your adult life[a] and they should have your ear on a crucial issue like a life mate, especially if they are praying for you. Need I point out that they have known you a very long time? That doesn't mean that the decision should be theirs. As we saw above, you are *leaving* them when you marry, and that begins with the decision *to* marry. If your parents are together and happy, you definitely want to hear why, but counterexamples also help us. Even if you do not admire your parents' marriage, they have already been through a lot and, again, if the relationship permits, they can share that understanding.

---

a. Exo 20:12; Deu 5:16; Pro 3:1–2; Pro 6:20–22; Mat 15:4; Mat 19:17–19; Eph 6:2.

God means parents to be a help to us, and I find that He is quite serious about this. Aubrey's father, Harry, was something of an independent Baptist — certainly not Pentecostal or charismatic in his Christian practice. So it was very disturbing to him when he started getting dreams that his daughter should not marry Mike, Aubrey's fiancé. Mike had even approached Harry and asked for his blessing, which he gave. Everything seemed rosy. It was awkward that now this very practical dad was walking around with this dark cloud over his head about this couple's future. Their family communication was not the best, so what should have been a heart-to-heart between Harry and Aubrey did not happen. Instead, she just noticed how terribly sad her dad had become. Eventually she found out that Harry just couldn't bring himself to bring it up with her. But that was *after* she had come to the awful conclusion herself that her engagement with Mike should end. Such a breakup is a heavy burden for a girl to carry by herself. It would have really helped her to have her father's assessment along with hers for the decision.

Parents can do poorly. They can panic when things get real. And there do exist selfish, worldly, and downright evil parents, who will give you terrible advice and try to sabotage you. Their advice needs your humble discernment. But most parents really do want their child's happiness. Some of us parents are better than others at prioritizing that desire for your best over other desires, but there are always valuable things to hear from those who have a long-term stake in your happiness. Their participation in your life will likely be longer than your current friends, so do your best to listen.

I once attended the wedding of Josh, a friend of a friend. At the festivities, the groom stood up and gave a heartfelt speech thanking those who had helped prepare him to reach this point of matrimony. It was a noble thought, wanting to thank his helpers. He enthused at how his friends, all his age and all single, had mentored him in this romance: "Thank you so much for coaching me about relationships and getting me to this point," Josh gushed. I noticed the groom's father sitting there looking a little annoyed at his son's speech. Then came the time for this father to speak. He stood up and said, "I think that Josh's friends are good guys, but it is curious that my son, in preparing for marriage, chose for his coaches men who have never played the game." This line met with a peal of laughter from all of us, especially from me. As an outside observer, I could enjoy the irony without any embarrassment. In spite of the family's discomfiture, the point was well taken.

Your pastor, too, has been placed in your life to help with his experience with relationships.ᵃ Perhaps he can help you more than I can. The one sadness of writing this book is realizing that I cannot address each situation personally. As a pastor, I know that every person's strengths and challenges and weaknesses and joys and struggles are at least a little different, and sometimes unique. In a book, I cannot possibly cover you as an individual. I am sorry for that. But what I can do—and this is the joy of writing this book—is show you the universal truths that govern relationship formation, truths that start to operate in dating.

---

a. Act 20:17; Act 28; Eph 4:11–15; Heb 13:17.

These principles put you so far ahead in terms of forming a lasting relationship that, in following them, you are almost guaranteed to not end up a divorce data point on the graphs printed above. With these truths, applied in the Holy Spirit, you can have a fantastic marriage. It doesn't matter who you are or where you are starting from.

I know because I have seen it in the stories I am going to tell you. And by the way, every story in this book is true. I have altered a few of the circumstances to protect the foolish. But they happened as described. Most of them are not uncommon. In fact, if you have lived a little while, you have probably seen some of these same stories play out among your own friends and family. They have helped me to see that these principles are enduring, that the Bible from which they are drawn once again proves itself true, and that God really does want our happiness.

A Steady Platform

As a pastor, I have tried very hard to help marriages start well. I have used many engagement and pre-marriage counseling books and programs. They all seek to prepare a dating couple for what lies ahead. They may ground their advice in spiritual principles, but there is also a drive to be practical, to get down to the nitty-gritty of living together. So the thinking goes, it is important to hit the four or five most popular points of conflict that couples face. There is usually one chapter on finances, one or two on conflict resolution, one on sex, one on relationships with the parents, one on children, and one, or many more, on communication skills.

Another approach administers a personality test of some sort to help a couple understand each other, whether it is their Myers-Briggs types, their DiSC scores, their love languages, or their Enneagram type. I have used many of these different approaches as I have done my pastoral best to prepare couples for the decision to become engaged and to marry. I have then watched the couples after the wedding, as the years go on. I have tried to note how they could have been better prepared. I got to be bothered by a few things.

The first step in sound preparation is simply realizing that we do not know what is coming in life. Newlyweds certainly don't know what is coming at them. I don't either. Will they lose the support of their families through some disagreement? Will they have a problem in bed? Is one of their careers about to skyrocket, leaving them confused about what their life together is about? Is a financial crisis about to rob them of all security? Will an unexpected windfall leave them rich and suddenly feeling like they don't know or need each other? Will the death of a child devastate them? Or will a long-hidden previous mistake that one of them has made resurface and leave the other suspicious of motives?

I began to realize something. What a couple really needs in the face of life's enormous uncertainty is a platform to withstand *any* problem or blessing, whether the difficulty arises from inside the relationship or outside of it. Whether the crisis comes at you from children or sex or money, whether confronted with unexpected catastrophe or sudden bonus, spouses need a pattern of movement toward each other that draws them closer in fair weather and foul. This way must go deeper than smart tips to remember when having conflicts. It must work for them, whatever their starting point, whether mature or immature. It must be flexible enough to encompass different personality types and life changes. Now such a steady platform would be some amazing and treasured thing, wouldn't it?

'Peas in a Pod,' or 'Opposites Attract'?

Compatibility testing as an approach contains another conundrum: there are all different kinds of matches in marriages. Back in university, friends would chuckle at this one couple that got together in my residential college. He was one of the tallest guys around. And she was tiny. We mused about how it might work physically. But laugh as we may, some terrific marriages are made of people who differ in almost every way. Others are composed of peas in a pod, so similar in their personalities that they never argue about where to go on vacation or what to do when they get there. God seems to have different points of affirmation and sanctification in each marriage. As I survey the matrimonial landscape, I see an almost infinite variety of complimentary combinations reflected in the eye of our Creator. It simply is not the case that certain kinds of people go best together.

Testing to determine compatibility can foster some helpful conversation. Sure. But as far as identifying the great obstacles you will face in marriage, sometimes it does. Often it does not. Marriage goes on for life, but personality and preferences change throughout life. This is frankly admitted by the tests themselves. Most tests encourage testing periodically, since the results for an individual, we are told, may change. So should we really judge our readiness for a lifetime on changeable results?

The same holds for judging the relationship by things you like to do together now. It turns out that both of you being fond of hip-hop music, or both of you adoring the outdoors, or both of you doing decathlons, or both having imbibed the same books, or being bored by board games, or hating the Seattle Seahawks, is not a reliable measure of how you will be together. These are not what your marriage will be about in ten years. They will not help you tackle the issues you will face.

Some daters admirably try to get everything out on the table ahead of time. They have a list of big issues to seek agreement on, and they try, early on, to talk about these to see if there is pairing with a potential partner: Where is it acceptable to live? How many children do you want? Do you like to travel? How do you feel about Reformed theology? And so on. This is not a bad idea, of course. It can be helpful. But it does not go deep enough because these things can also change through life. Some confirmed opinions, such as the number of children you want, can swing radically depending on the experiences you have. Don't ever, ever ask a woman, for example, if she wants another child right after she has given birth. One dating couple received a book of a hundred questions to discuss before getting married. A hundred? They only got through five of them before they married, moved, and lost the book. Based on what I see in their marriage today, I can tell you that they didn't need the other ninety-five.

More helpful is knowing how to agree or disagree and still move toward each other. Because marriage takes us so deeply into confronting who we are and who our spouse is, we need to somehow embark on a deep enough discussion to start us down the road of mutual trust. And we need to begin that discussion ahead of time, at the beginning, when we are dating.

I am going to let you in on a secret. It may sound sneaky, but the first thing I do when I accept a couple for engagement counseling is get down on my knees and start to pray that they will have a conflict. I pray that God will bring them into disagreement. I pray this especially for the ones that come into my office saying, "We never argue! That is what is so amazing about our relationship." For a pastor to pray this may sound a bit off. I don't pray this because I am mean, but because they need a depth of discussion that shows them something important amidst disagreement. I want them to see how they can face and overcome even that heartbreaking moment of serious distance. That moment will come when it feels like there is no solution at all, when all appears to be in jeopardy.

But I am getting ahead of myself. The point is that these observations led me toward a different approach in meeting with engaged and dating couples. While the other approaches outlined above can be helpful—principally in getting people to talk to each other—beginning couples need a stronger foundation. If compatibility testing or big-issue discussions or conflict techniques or pass-time pairing don't do it, what does? What could provide this powerful platform? Enter the Bible.

Love Is an Intergendered Thing

In the Scriptures we have advice that has stood the test of thousands of years. When properly contextualized, we find principles designed for life in any culture, at any time, in any place. So I simply started to highlight for daters what the Bible considers important in marriage.

And what does the Bible highlight about marriage? Though the New Testament talks plenty about sex and money and communication, when its writers focus on marriage, that is not what they feel compelled to get across. Instead, they talk about gender.

When I use the word *gender* and point out that the Bible emphasizes it in relationship, I am not talking about society-constructed roles or cultural expectations. I mean that the Bible describes a shape to our souls that is reflected in our male and female bodies, binary and beautiful. Paying attention to gender in relationship is what makes a marriage bloom because it operates on such a deep level in people. Intergendered love not only enables a couple to survive; it increases intimacy between them.[a] Then it produces fruit that goes beyond them, the most obvious being children,[b] and makes a refuge of good for others. The guidance of this gift sets up a couple to

---

a. Eph 5:22–33.
b. Mal 2:5; Gen 1:28.

respond to each other in any crisis they face or any need that they meet. It's the platform.

That is why this book is also only for intergendered relationships. In our world, some opt for a monogendered relationships, sometimes called same-sex unions. But as I explain in another book I wrote called *enGendered*, romantic, monogendered relationships are not God's way for those who call on the name of Christ. If you are someone who has same-sex attraction, that is not the end for you though. You should know that an intergendered marriage is still quite possible for you, as is apparent in some of the following stories.

This is also a book for those who accept the masculine and feminine as real and created features of our selves. These days, many tend to believe that masculine or feminine is a person's personal decision based on their own understanding of themselves. Others simply doubt gender's existence. But the Scriptures direct us to celebrate woman and man as a glorious part of what it is to be made in God's image. *Made* here means that you do not choose your gender based on your inner feelings. You are directed to it by your body. And I can tell you that when you look into the Bible's pages about it, its counsel will often surprise you.

For example, the Bible doggedly resists listing man's and woman's innate qualities. We tend to define masculinity and femininity by traits, but the Bible never does. After saying that men and women are different,[a] none of the prophets of the sixty-six books ventures the charac-

---

a. Gen 5:2.

teristics (or even one characteristic) that makes a woman a woman, or a man a man.[27] It is not as if the writers do not talk about men and women, describe men and women, instruct men as men and women as women. But in getting down to profound basics, which the Bible always seems to do, there is a resolute silence on manly or womanly attributes. Instead, it talks about what they do for one another. Why? It is because the meaning of gender is found in relationships. Certainly, we are different, and our bodies are given to point out the difference, and show us the shape of our souls,[a] but we men find our masculinity in the company of close women, and we women, our femininity in the interaction with close men. The meaning of gender is that men and women love each other differently.

Do you wonder what made the difference between Alan's story and Jake's story that began this chapter, with their compass-point princesses? I was close to both men and watched their stories unfold from the beginning. I can tell you that Alan allowed a kind of holy gendered testing in dating Amber. But Jake did not. Alan asked questions similar to the ones in Parts II & III. But Jake did not. If you are impatient, you can skip right to Part II and get going on those questions. There is no problem in doing that. But if you can hold out a little more for some background, it may help you to understand what you are asking. Because before we start asking these twelve questions, I would like you to see whence they come.

---

a. Gen 2:7; Jam 2:26.

Four

An Ancient Secret

*I do not understand what a post-gender world is, or would
be, or why we would even want it. Sounds boring.*
— Mitchell Davis [28]

*As a lily among brambles,
so is my love among the young women.
As an apple tree among the trees of the forest,
so is my beloved among the young men.*
— The Bridegroom and the Bride [a]

You don't live long enough to learn from experience.
— Jewish proverb

The First Romantic Comedy

The Bible pretty much begins with a romantic comedy
about two single people. After that initial Chapter setting
up all the scenery (Genesis 1), it jumps into a story of
longing and release to rival anything that Katherine Heigl
or Ryan Gosling ever did. The great drama that is Genesis
2 begins with a loner guy. He is earthy and silent and
dedicated to what he does best: his work. But you can tell
that something is missing in his life. If this were a movie,
there would probably be a funny scene of Adam awk-
wardly trying to tell his problems to a cow and getting a
blank stare. The guy goes through various machinations,
embarks on a few side stories, and experiences a wounding
trauma. The girl, meanwhile, arrives fresh and innocent
and unprepared for what is coming. Though neither of

---

a. Sos 2:2–3.

them realize it, she has a connection to him in her past
that will ultimately tie them together. Then, at last—what
we hoped for—they meet. The guy stammers out some
sweaty thoughts, but from that moment on, you know
that they will be together ever after. A final generalization
about marriage is proclaimed to wrap up the scene and the
Chapter fades to black. Besides warming your heart, this
story can make you a wise dater.

The Stone the Builders Rejected

The people of our time are rapidly leaving behind the
gender wisdom of the ages. It lies strewn along the side
of the relationship road like precious jewels, discarded in
a great rush to reinvent the way we come together using
mere cardboard and Scotch Tape. One can trace this
folly of innovation back to Genesis 3 when, after the first
couple rejected God's good desire for them, He outlined
their new reality:[a] "Your desire will be for [to master] your
husband and he will rule [harshly] over you."[29] From then
on, as Adam and Eve's sons and daughters rebelled against
God's way, we moved forward through abuse and manip-
ulation *en masse* to our times. Today, society's solution to
the gender conflict is to simply deny that men and women
(that is, gender) even exist beyond a personal preference.
It's not a great solution.

Of course, the meaning of gender and gender differences is controversial, but we must speak about them if we
are speaking about relationships. Because gender is about

---

a. Gen 3:16 (NIV).

relationship. And close romantic relationships are about gender. As soon as God decided to make us in His image, He determined us to have gendered relationships.

Many people have read Genesis 1:27: "So God created man in his own image, in the image of God he created him; male and female He created them," and wondered what that means. What constitutes the great *imago dei* in us? What is it that separates us from animals and angels? The different ways through history that Christians have understood the image of God in us boil down to basically three.[30]

Early in church history, theologians listed the attributes of God and how we share them. God has things like omniscience, kindness, and a will; we also know some things, can be kind, and want to do some stuff and not other stuff. Some of God's attributes were deemed not shareable (incommunicable) and some we could take part in (communicable), but it was thought that we partake in divine attributes to some extent, and that is what makes us the image of God. Probably there is truth to this interpretation. Augustine did a twist on this when he located an analogy of the Trinity in our individual minds (memory, thought, and will).

But later people decided that defining something by its attributes was a very Greek way of thinking, and probably not shared by the original audience of these words of Genesis. Biblical theologians pointed out how ancient kings would set up statues of themselves all over their empires. The artwork showed dominion over their territory. You would see one of these images of the king and say, "Yikes, Ozymandias is in charge of this area. I should look on him and fear." Moses's ancient Near Eastern audience would most likely understand *image* this way. Accordingly, what immediately follows in the passage is God explaining His creation of this image to "exercise dominion" over all that He made.[a] This means we are like those statues, highly upgraded of course, filling up the earth as under-stewards of God's good works. Ruling the earth, then, is what it means to be made in His image. Again, this reading has good support and probably has some truth to it.

But a third understanding arose, as theologians went back and read what the verse itself actually says, especially in light of the revelation of the New Testament about who God is. In making man in His image, God made man "male and female"; that is, being in the image of God means being in, and being able to be in, close, gendered covenantal relationships. This brings us back to the curious features of the great Genesis 2 romantic comedy.

A Deep Identity

What is the first thing that Sleepless-in-Seattle Adam does, after he gets over his shock at Eve? He names her. He says, "She shall be called 'Woman.'"[b] As we will elaborate further on, with this act Adam is acting with authority, mission, and care. He gives Eve a place to know herself.

The meaning of the name Adam gives to Eve is hugely important for Eve to understand who she is as a

---

a. Gen 1:28–30.
b. Gen 2:23.

woman. In Hebrew she is אִשָּׁה (*ishah*), derived from אִישׁ (*ish*), the word for *man*. It is a name that summarizes how she was made, being "taken out of" him. It is a gutsy way of saying that she was equal to Adam because she was made of the same stuff. That equality set her apart from the animals, which were found inadequate to help the man.[a] Okay, those things seem "genderly" meaningful, but how deep does that meaning go?

This second Chapter of Genesis is elaborating on how God performed His stated act of creating His image in Chapter 1. As we've noted, He does it by creating gender. After making a guy, God says that it is not good for this one person to be alone. Somehow, that doesn't fit the reality of God. So, He puts the guy to sleep and engages in a brutal operation, removing some of his structural insides, a rib, from which the woman, Eve, is formed.[b] Hence, Adam's initial description of her, of being taken out of him, when they meet.

But ask yourself something: *Why do it this way?* There are many ways God could have made the woman. Mixing clay and baking her in some primordial oven;[31] having her spring whole-cloth from the head of the guy;[32] making her first and then, when He saw her, starting over to make the man.[33] But He chooses this bloody, invasive act on the man instead. Why?

It would seem, listening to rabbis and preachers, that God only did it this way to provide fodder for wedding sermons. For example, "God didn't take from the head

---

a. Gen 2:20.
b. Gen 2:22–23.

of Adam, or Eve would dominate him, or from the foot
of Adam or he would stomp on her, but from the side,
so they would be partners..." and so on. Such midrash
makes for a nice ceremony. But this is a brutal act. And
God is never arbitrary in brutal acts. Come to think of it,
God is never arbitrary, period. He always has a point.

At a key moment in church history, Gregory of
Nazianzus recognized the point in Eve's "of-ness."
Gregory was part of the fourth-century movement to
define orthodox doctrine about God for the church and
he relates it to gender in a sermon he preached at the
time. Gregory says that, while Eve is a distinct person,
she is made of what Adam is made of. He says that Eve is
homoousios as Adam.[34] If that word, meaning "of the same
substance," reminds you of something, then you have
the point. In AD 325, the same year Gregory gave that
sermon, at the Council of Nicaea (one of the most important meetings ever held), the church decided that this term
was how we should talk about God. As Christians we
understand God to be one God and yet three Persons.[a]
Homoousios, it was decided at Nicaea, was a good term
to describe the Members of this Trinity, specifically the
first Two. The great Sent One,[b] whom we came to know
as Jesus Christ, was of the same substance as the Almighty
Sender. Adam and Eve are like the first two Persons of
the Trinity, from Whose union comes a Third, also of the
same substance.

---

a. Mat 28:19; Rom 5:1-8; Gal 4:4-6; Eph 1:3-14; 2Co 13:13; Rev 1:4-5. Jesus is our God
   (2Pe 1:1), and all three Divine Persons are oriented toward each other (2Pe 1:16-21).
b. Mar 9:37; Luk 9:48; Luk 10:16; Joh 5:38; Joh 7:18; Joh 9:4; Joh 10:36; Joh 13:16; Joh
   13:20; Joh 17:18; 1Jo 4:9.

Is not God saying just this when He says, "Let *us*[35] make man in Our image... male and female"?[a] The image, like the Speaker, is both plural and singular. If God is trying to show in Chapter 2 what He had just declared in Chapter 1 — that something in the relationship and difference between the male and the female makes the image of God — this would be it. Eve with her own equal personhood is yet one with Adam in bone and flesh: an equality and plurality in unity. And she proceeds from him. This "of the same substance, proceeding from" point seems to be the idea in Adam's mind when He sees Eve for the first time. His big first thought is that she is "bone of my bones and flesh of my flesh, because she was taken out of" me.[b] And then God has the two "multiply," so there is a third.[c]

Of course, God differs from us in big ways. We are only an image. But when we come together in close relationship, we mirror the Trinity's Persons, God "Themself." That is why we have friendship, why we have families and churches, and especially why we go on dates and get married.

The Heavenly Relationship [36]

You may find talk about the Holy Trinity confusing. You may ask, *Why do we need to talk about worshiping one God in Trinity, Trinity in Unity, and how the three Persons are coequal and coeternal and all that?* It just ties your mind up in knots. Or, as the Clint Eastwood character,

---

a. Gen 1:26 (emphasis mine).
b. Gen 2:23.
c. Gen 1:28.

Frankie Dunn, mocked in the movie, *Million Dollar Baby*, "Is the Trinity like those three cartoon characters on the cereal box — Snap, Crackle, Pop?"[37] In other words, is God just like Rice Krispies?

If you are ever going to begin to understand the New Testament's teaching on the Trinity, how these three Persons are one God, the first thing you need to know is that They are crazy about each Other. I mean, crazy. They talk about each Other all the time. They think about each Other all the time. They do things for each Other all the time. This is most clearly seen in the New Testament among the first two Persons. In the Gospel of Luke, for example, Jesus Christ's first words spoken and last words spoken are a reference to "my Father."[a] And so much of what Jesus says in between is about that same Father. When the Latter explicitly shows up in the Gospels, it is to express how He feels about His "Beloved."[b] The One is so into the Other that They actually indwell each Other. If you have never looked closely at how prevalent the Trinity is in the Bible, and how often the different Members, when They are distinguished, focus on One Another, it would pay to get a good book that tours the subject.[38] By the time you get through this kind of demonstration, seeing how They dote on One Another, you are liable to wonder how God has any time for us at all.[39]

It is not only our human father-son relationship that reflects the Trinity. The Bible switches the family metaphor for the Trinity in several places because no

---

a. Luk 2:49; Luk 24:49.
b. Mat 3:17; Mat 17:5; with parallels: Mar 1:11; Luk 3:22; Mar 9:7, a practice begun long before: Isa 42:1.

single analogy captures God. The apostle Paul relates the Genesis 1–2 creation narrative to gender at least ten times in his letters to the churches![40] He must have thought a lot about gender and the interpretation of human origins. The result was his conviction that we should look for gender's archetype in God. We are to understand masculinity and femininity as coming "out of God."[a]

That is why we can understand the Trinity better when we start dating. Our man-woman relationships find their passionate archetype in what goes on in the first two of God's Persons. (Appendix II explains this archetype further.) The exhilaration we feel on a great date is a little bit of the bliss They have all the time. So, it is not surprising when the apostle Paul, while discussing gender relations, compares the incarnate Christ and the Almighty to a wife and husband, saying,

> I want you to understand that the head of every man is Christ, the head of a wife is her husband, and the head of Christ is God.[b]

Some restrict this analogy to only Christ's time on earth as a man, or limit its applicability in showing us the Trinity *in se* (as the Persons really are in Themself), but as we discuss below in chapter 6, doing so raises the question of why Christ was the one trinitarian Person to take on the earthly mission of being sent. The statement must still speak to us about the trinitarian relationship. It is no secret that the feeling of being loved and loving powered

---

a. 1Co 11:12.
b. 1Co 11:3.

the life of Jesus Christ. Only it wasn't a love with another
human being. It was this love with the Almighty Head.
The electrifying passion between Them is what makes
periodic movie and book conjectures that Jesus had a
wife or was secretly married to Mary Magdalene so funny
(think *The da Vinci Code, The Last Temptation of Christ,
Habit,* etc.), as if that would be a need or a big temptation
for Him. Such an idea is simply comical compared to the
reality of Christ's love with the Head (the Father) that we
see in the Gospels.

In saying this, Paul is not saying that God is exactly
like our marriages. We wouldn't say that the Persons of
the Trinity are married. God is utterly unique. He is so far
above us and goes on forever and ever. But He does give
us true knowledge about God in Themself.[41] And what
we do in biblical marriage imitates what God does.[42] God
freely chose to share some measure of His inter-relation-
ship with us. Somehow when He mapped the image of
His processions onto creation, it came out as male and
female, from the union of which proceeds a Third. (The
creational meaning of the Third, the Holy Spirit, for our
relationships is taken up in chapter 10).

That is why gender will continue to work among us,
even in a culture such as ours that is doing its darnedest
to dismiss it. Dominic, a longtime friend of mine, made
the difficult and expensive decision a few years back to
assume a new name, partially transition, and begin living
as a woman. I offered cautions at the time, knowing that
the reality of gender can only be contradicted at great personal cost. Taking imitative hormones, amputating sexual

organs and performing cosmetic surgery, commonly
called "transitioning," has not been shown to reduce the
high rate of suicide attempts among adults who choose
to identify with a gender opposite that of their body.[43]
But someone with Dominic's difficulties in our cultural
context is now unlikely to be dissuaded from such a
course of action. Was all lost? Well, Dominic emailed me
a few months ago to inform me: "After an elaborate ruse
by my girlfriend, she and I just got engaged!" I know
something of my friend's needs. That relationship was
a healthy step, so I could rejoice with him. Though not
so in his mind, I saw a hurting boy who had love with a
girl. I wrote back: "Hey, that is wonderful news. Con-
gratulations! I wish you every happiness." And I meant it.
Because, however rudimentary, gender was at work.

Through the glass darkly, intergendered relationship,
as it is explained in the Scriptures and born out in our
lives, reveals our triune God. So also, as Paul teaches, the
comparison with us helps us love. When we learn of God,
we see how to pursue marriage. This fact gives us great
wisdom in how to date.

Christ Our Paragon

As with all things in life, we connect with God through
His supreme revelation in the world—that is, Jesus Christ.
Christ is our one mediator[a] and our example as people.[b]
He fills all things and is preeminent in all things.[c] So Christ

---

a. 1Ti 2:5.
b. 1Co 11:1.
c. Eph 1:23; Eph 4:10.

is our model as men for our relationships. Adam, the first man, is given to marry Eve. This is because God likewise takes a masculine role with His people, at times describing Himself as their bridegroom or husband.[a] Jesus Christ was God become man, born as the masculine. As we saw in chapter 1, He too uses the metaphor of marital engagement, with Himself as the bridegroom, to help us respond to Him in hope and love. The New Testament apostles follow suit in identifying the followers of Christ as His bride.[b] As we look at Christ and the way that He treats, and is treated, by the church, it helps us to see how to be real men in a relationship with a woman.

But Christ is not just a paragon for men being men. He has first place in all things,[c] including women being women. How would Christ be an inspiration for women in relationship? Recall that the meaning of gender is found in relationship. Sometimes it is appropriate, from a different perspective, to understand Christ as feminine to God.[44] In some key trinitarian passages,[d] the second Member of the Trinity is called the Beloved One.[e] Likewise, the first Member of the Trinity is characterized by the promises He habitually makes to the Beloved,[45] and could be appropriately named, the Promiser. These biblical names help us see the archetype of gender in the Trinity. Just as Eve was equal with Adam yet a distinct person begotten from him, so the Beloved One is of one substance with the Promiser and yet a distinct Person Who is eternally of Him. So,

a. Jer 31:32.
b. Joh 3:28–30; Eph 5:31–32; Rev 19:6–9; Rev 21:2–4.
c. Col 1:18.
d. Eph 1:3–23; Isa 42:1–8.
e. Eph 1:6; Isa 42:1: "in whom my soul delights."

from some vantage points, Christ shows us the feminine via that relationship.

For example, the Old Testament gives us the character of Woman Wisdom, feminine *in relation to* the Lord, and her pre-incarnation conversation with Him, to help us understand that dimension of the Beloved, or second trinitarian Person, in relationship to the Promiser, or first trinitarian Person.[a] "Wisdom has built her house" and claims that at the time of creation, "I was constantly beside [the Lord]... and I was daily his delight, rejoicing before him always."[b]

That Beloved then became known to us in incarnate form as Jesus Christ. When Christ, in His teaching, identifies with the Old Testament Woman Wisdom[c] or when He identifies with a feminine role,[d] He is using the lens of intergendered relationship to say that the Beloved can be seen as feminine *in relation to* the Promiser. As we saw above, Paul follows suit in telling us that both genders come out of God[e] and likening Christ with God to a wife with her husband in marriage.[f] When we see how the Beloved treats, and is treated by, the Promiser in a covenantal relationship, we understand where womanliness comes from and how to be a true woman with a man. Christ is there for both man and woman. This is why, in 1 Corinthians 11:3 quoted above, Christ is said to be both the head of all of us (masculine) *as well as* "headed

---

a. Pro 8:1–9:12.
b. Pro 8:30.
c. Mat 11:19; Luk 7:34–35.
d. Mat 23:37; Luk 13:34.
e. 1Co 11:11–12: all things (the masculine and feminine) are "out of" God.
f. 1Co 11:3.

by" God the Father (feminine). Both of us are meant to become like Christ in our genders.

Now, metaphors have limits, and this neglected one can be interpreted and misinterpreted in different ways. So how do we know in what way we should follow Christ's example as a bridegroom, or how to be like Christ as the Beloved of God? The failsafe way to do this is through the norms of Scripture. We interpret these metaphors through the Bible's commands and the principles from its narratives to know how to follow the Christ in our genders. This brings us to the definitive reading of gender in the Genesis 2 romantic comedy, given to us by the apostle Paul, along with the keys to date well.

The Apostle Paul's Fashion Sense

The principles underlying our work in dating come from Paul's reading of the first coming together of a man with a woman. He identifies three differences between the original thrust of woman and man that undergird how they love each other differently. We can call these asymmetries, and we can see them laid out in the famous gender passage about head coverings in Paul's letter to the Corinthians.[a]

The apostle Paul instructs the church at Corinth to respect their first-century Roman cultural expressions of gender distinction. He is specifically speaking about when they come together for public worship. Clothing is always a way to make a statement about identity. You know this when you are preparing to go out, right? Which dress says

a. 1Co 11:2–16.

the right thing about you to your date? Which jeans or shoes say, *"Me* as I should be seen"? Paul recognizes that this is always true about clothes, even when people go to church, and tells us to use it, to use our cultural practices to practice gender.

The way to do gender publicly in the first-century Roman Empire clothing was through head coverings. When married women at that time went out in public, they would cover their heads with a kind of hoodie, to show their relationship to their husband. This is well-documented by the graves, statues and reliefs of the period.[46] Some examples from the art of this Roman period are shown below.

Clockwise from top left: Wife of Damas Gravestone, Hierapolis / Bust of Married Woman, Antalya Museum / Woman from Perge, Antalya Museum / Sarcophagus of Aurelia Botaiane and Demetria from Perge, Antalya Museum / Sarcophagus of Hercules, Konya

Well, some of the nouveau riche of the up-and-coming city of Corinth were challenging this traditional practice, and it was a big deal. They wrote to Paul about it, asking for his judgment. Paul comes down decidedly on the side of those who wanted to keep up the cultural tradition. He is very clear that they should continue to wear head coverings. Why would he do this if it was just some societal norm? The apostle wisely advises using the cultural tradition to make the point that men and women approach each other in distinct ways. Paul is adamant that the Christians of Corinth should stand against their culture when that culture tries to minimize gender. This might well be a useful lesson also for Christians in other cultures to come after ancient Rome.

While clarifying the controversy, Paul makes his definitive statement of gender asymmetry.[a] The passage both begins and ends with the statement of what married couples ought to do with regard to their heads. Verse 7: the man ought *not to* cover his head. Verse 10: the woman ought *to* cover her head:

[7] *For a man ought not to cover his head,*

> *since he is the image and glory of God, but woman is the glory of man.*

> [8] *For man was not made from woman, but woman from man.*

> [9] *Neither was man created for woman, but woman for man.*

---

a. 1Co 11:7-10.

[10] *That is why a wife ought to have a symbol of authority on her head.*

These verses form what is called in literary circles an *inclusio*—that is, a repetition of words and concepts that mark off the beginning and ending of a paragraph, tying together the thoughts inside. Inside this *inclusio*, in between the man/woman "ought" statements about their heads, Paul gives his reasons from his reading of Genesis 2, delineating three asymmetries between women and men in relationship. In the original Greek, there are three repetitions of "for not/neither" (γὰρ οὐκ, *gar ouk*), giving us three "because" clauses: because one is the glory of the other; because one is made from the other; and because they are made for different purposes in God's work. These three give us the shape of intergendered love.

Different Shapes for Different Loving

Let us look briefly at Paul's three asymmetries to get a framework for our dating questions.

Verse 7 — An asymmetry of order. Both men and women are created in the image of God, so they are equal in showing us God. That is why, in the second half of the sentence, Paul does not say "woman is the *image* of man." That would be heretical. Woman is the *image of God*, just as man is.[a] Instead he says that woman is just the *glory* of man (or "a man"). Varying the phrases, subtracting the "image" part from the woman's relation to man, the apostle

---

a. Gen 1:27; Num 6:2-3. They are capable of equal devotion.

is intentionally expressing the equality of men and women.

Yet they were created in a different sequence. Because one, the firstborn, so to speak, was created first, the second becomes "the glory of" the first in a unique way.[47] To give someone glory is to make them important. As she esteems him, promotes him, basically makes him look good, he in turn uses that status for her. She offers him the responsibility of the firstborn. He assumes that responsibility for her benefit and growth. Paul soon after in his letter applies this gender principle again while explaining[48] the order of church worship.[a]

Verse 8 — An asymmetry of origin. Women and men are created in a different way. God got his hands dirty in both cases, but He used a different building program when he set to work on the woman than when he bent down in the dust and scooped together the man.[b] Thus, when they come together, there are some different things that they do for each other. Some of the things they do for one another are the same, like providing a date on Friday night or driving the other when sick to the hospital. But there are also some deep, differently shaped gifts with which they serve one another. As he secures her, she gives him rest. As he grounds her in love, she brings him home.

Verse 9 — An asymmetry of intent. God always has a mission for a relationship. He means marriages to further His kingdom on earth. The original man and woman were created for different tasks in that mission.[c] She powers the mission with which he is commissioned. The imprint

---

a. 1Co 14:29–35.
b. Gen 2:7; Gen 2:22.
c. Gen 2:15; Gen 2:18.

of those differences continues to determine how to move forward in the purposes of the relationship. Living in this asymmetry keeps a couple focused on God's purposes rather than on one or the other of their careers.

These three enduring principles do not just pop up in this passage. They are found throughout the Bible.[49] For they are the platform of marriage. So they serve us well to be adapted as questions in this book for determining a lifetime mate.

A Reliable Rock

In recent years, the church has participated in the culture's denigration of gender. Emphasizing the important truth of the *equality* of women and men, the culture lost the other important truth that God decreed *asymmetry* between His image-bearers. Relationship is what gender is about. If there is not any difference between men and women in relationship, why would you need one or the other in intimate unions? Thus, gender minimization in marriage leads to gayness, but that is not where gender deconstruction stops. The current transgender movement and growing widespread gender dysphoria were entirely predictable. When people don't know who they are in relationship, they start to lose what it is to be a man or to be a woman. They buy in to superficial cultural stereotypes, all the while sensing that these are not the real thing. They then decide that they don't fit in and don't need to. Gender dysphoria will continue to increase for this simple reason. When you lose gender in relationship, you lose gender.

A strong relationship starts in staying close to the Scriptures in navigating masculinity and femininity. There we find that men and women love each other differently. To reject this truth of gender is to forego that intimacy and fruitfulness with which our marriages were meant to brim. As cultural tides and academic theories wash in and wash out, the Bible remains a reliable rock. When you put your weight on it, it does not budge or give or even wiggle a little. And, when trying to date with so much on the line, when trying to make the dangerous decision, that rock is exactly what we need for our platform.

Of course, we could decide to reinvent ourselves and make up our own rules of interpersonal interactions. But relationships are so important that it takes years to evaluate decisions we made about how we treated another person. Their real import takes a lifetime to crystallize. As the Jewish proverb says, "You don't live long enough to learn from experience." You can get to the end of your life and look back and see if you did it right. But if you did it wrong, which is easy to do, you will have riddled a life with pain—yours, and probably several others.

Prototyping

I talk in this book about principles for dating, and yet I draw them from passages about marriage. This might bother you. Can't we lighten up? Going on a date is far from baby seats and life-insurance policies with long-term care riders. You don't feel at all ready, and maybe not even interested, in all that down-the-road stuff. So why talk about marriage when talking about dating?

How you date is laying a foundation for your marriage—whether you want it to or not. Remember in chapter 3 George's realization that his marriage failure with Francis began at the beginning of their dating? Do you recall how Alan's and Jake's marriages were made in how they dated? As we discussed there, how you handle all that down-the-road stuff begins with how you treat your date. I am not saying that we do not grow through our lives along with our partners. You can tell from some of the personal stories I am sharing in this book that I had a lot of growing to do back when I was dating. I had a long way to go to become some semblance of a man. Indeed, we should not expect to be ready for all of life when we're just going with someone to play pool or to pass the evening at the pub. We have time to learn other things we may need to face the challenges of children and two-car garages. But the nature of relationships is such that they always grow from a history. How they begin remains forever part of the relationship. How you handle yourself with one another is building something from the get-go, like it or not. Something good or bad. Sound or faulty.

So, your dating relationship is a prototype. Ideally, dating should be fun. It can be if you are confident about what you are doing. And while you are having fun you are seeing if you are becoming one flesh, without really being one flesh yet.

One more thing before we begin. I hope that this chapter has shown you how Christianity gives us deep answers about relationships. In fact, only Christianity explains why they are so essential to our lives: because

of the plurality in the unity of God—distinct Persons
in relationship make up the One, and so we mirror
that. Islam cannot say that. Neither can Judaism. In the
monistic religions of the East, Hinduism and Buddhism,
we are exhorted to get beyond human relationships to
reach enlightenment. A materialistic worldview also falls
short. Evolutionary hypotheses for the preference of
sexual reproduction over asexual (whether it developed
in prokaryotes or eukaryotes) are always embarrassingly
contrived. No other worldview can explain why we have
relationships and why they are so important. In any other
life philosophy, relationships are arbitrary. In Christianity
you have a robust reason for going on a date: because you
are the image of God. So you, Christian—of all people—
are equipped to make a wise dangerous decision. You can
do this right.

Part II
Is This the One?

This is not a book for married people. While wedded folk may find some useful marriage principles herein, such people differ in one very big way: They are no longer contestants in this dating game. You are yet in the realm of decision. You need some different counsel. To care for your date and yourself, you should be determining, with steel nerves, whether you two should make that journey over the mountain of infatuation to the valleys beyond of living together. Or not. One thing you must never do is get married just to get married. The answer to poor marriage statistics is not to push more people into marriage. Nor is it to cohabitate or to put off the whole enterprise for ten years. Instead, the answer is for those dating to have high standards.

Part I explained that marriage begins way before the marriage with deciding whom to marry. Marriage begins with choosing well by dating well. The question in the title above does not mean that there is only one person out there that you could or should marry. But it does mean having standards by which to test a potential mate. This may seem cold or calculating to you. You might think, *Can't we just spend time together and see if it works?* What I am proposing is that you do two things: enjoy your time together *while* you are measuring this may-be-mate. We inevitably do this measuring anyway, don't we? The servant of Abraham had a test to find a bride for Isaac.[a] The mother of King Lemuel rates qualities in looking for a good wife.[b] So let's have standards and be thoughtful about what exactly we are measuring.

But what standards? In some tribes of Borneo, even into the twentieth century, a man needed to behead an enemy to be eligible for marriage. I think we can pass on that one. Some people look for "love at first sight" or, the soft version of that principle, "I knew it from the first date." That is nice when it happens. But it is not *the* sign that you should be together. We would be unwise to place too much weight on that first-date feeling.

Other standards may make finding a mate improbable— such as, he must make this amount of money or she must have these physical measurements. Instead, have wise standards and allow these other things to take their rightful place as preferences, perhaps even strong preferences, but not deal-breakers, things that you would like but not the determinants of moving forward with the relationship. Because money or measurements or magical moments (I know this is hard to believe) will not keep your marriage together.

Let's make use of your dates. Besides grabbing a good time, experiencing the euphoria of falling in love, and luxuriating in no longer having to stand alone at parties, let's make your dates count. Let's make sure your dates are moving you somewhere, toward the goal of sober commitment or affectionate parting with gratitude for lessons learned, as we saw in chapter 1.

The test I offer you is a mere twelve questions: six

---

a. Gen 24:1–27.
b. Pro 31:30.

for guys, six for gals. You will get three questions to ask about her or him and three questions to ask about yourself. Part II (chapters 5–7) focuses on the other person. Part III (chapters 8–10) focuses on you. Seems easy enough, right? The questions are phrased as "Can he/she/I do this thing: X?" That is simple, right? No big deal. I could have phrased the questions as, "*Does* he/she/I do this thing?" But instead, I ask it the first way because sometimes the ability is not there yet, but the potential is. And that may be enough.

Here, then, are three tests of your relationship:

The Asymmetry of Origin — If you are the guy, ask if she brings you rest, perhaps in a way you haven't known before. Can her words, her deeds, or simply her presence be a home for you? If you are the woman, ask if he makes you secure in what he does, or if you think he could.

The Asymmetry of Order — As a woman, ask if he takes charge for your care and development. Is he able to step forward in responsibility for your sake? As a man, do you think she can honor you? Can she put you forward as a head? Is she ever able to surrender prerogative to you?

The Asymmetry of Intent — As a woman, you should ask if this man can lead in the mission you will have together. Can he find out why it is that God brought you together and what you should be doing for the Kingdom of heaven on earth? Likewise, as a man, you should ask if this woman has the divine spark to move your co-mission forward? Can she fit and empower what you see as God's standout purposes?

Let's look at how these questions work, to help you evaluate your date as you are dating. Ask the questions that are going to matter in the long-term. Dating is a genderly quest. Guard the gold. Don't sell yourself short.

Five

Can He Secure Me? / Can She Give Me Rest?

If if there were a drug, some voodoo, any kind of mind-altering magic remedy to keep the man intact, that would have been preferable.
—Dr. Renée Richards [50] (born Richard Raskind)

Eve...O fairest of creation! last and best
Of all God's works, Creature in whom excell'd
Whatever can to sight or thought be formed,
Holy, divine, good, amiable, or sweet!
— John Milton [51]

For Women: All That You Can Ask of Any Man

Billy Joel's breakthrough pop music album, *Piano Man*, certified Platinum in the US four times over, propelled him to stardom and made him a musician spokesman in the 1970s. The album filled America with relationship advice at that time. One of the songs swells these words to a woman:

> If I only had the words to tell you
> If you only had the time to understand
> But I only have these arms to hold you
> And it's all that you can ask of any man!

It is not surprising that Billy Joel never won any awards

for relationship-building. Beginning his first marriage on adultery with another man's wife and divorcing three times following, I think we can forego the musician's advice on relationships, however well-sung. Especially here. You can and should expect a lot more from a man than just two arms to hold you. Maybe you crave that, but you shouldn't settle for that. Your culture's gender disintegration stifles this call of men to do something much more for the women in their lives, but you don't have to.

In fact, according to the Bible, times have gotten really bad when society allows men to have women without a covenant or any promise of security. Really bad. When the prophet Isaiah begins his very difficult ministry of telling the Israelites that they will be going into exile in Assyria, he gives an overview of how bad things will be. Fools will be in charge,[a] wide-scale oppression will prevail over the land,[b] social conditions will be like Sodom,[c] and, perhaps worst of all, women will go deprived.[d] In fact:

> Seven women shall take hold of one man in that day, saying, "We will eat our own bread and wear our own clothes, only let us be called by your name; take away our reproach."[e]

Israel will hit rock bottom, proclaims Isaiah, when women will have to settle for a guy with "only these arms to hold you!"

---

a. Isa 3:4–6.
b. Isa 3:5; Isa 3:14–15.
c. Isa 3:9.
d. Isa 3:18–26.
e. Isa 4:1.

* * *

Electricity charged the atmosphere whenever Alice and her friends started talking about dating. There was enough ambiguity between them that it could not yet be told if one might match up with another. Have you ever been in a room like that? I feel at those times like I might get a shock just by touching the coffee table. One time, Alice took the charged opportunity to give her opinion about some things she felt she needed from a guy long-term. As an artist, she knew her earning power was not very high.

Liam said, hypothetically, "I'm not going to work in a factory so that you can be an artist, Alice."

"Fair enough," she countered, but she wondered what will happen when she has a child. "I just want to know what I can expect."

Another time, Xavier stopped the conversation with, "You don't have a right to expect anything from a guy, Alice, except to get along. That's all you can claim when you get together with someone."

Alice made a mental note: *When I do get together with someone, it won't be either of those two.*

When I heard about these conversations, my respect for Alice grew. She understood she had a right to expect more from a guy than "just getting along." She also knew that a guy had a right to expect a lot more from her as well.

Great Expectations

The first woman ever who bore God's image, our illustrious mother Eve, had this to expect from Adam: he

names her. He gives her a place to know herself. Boy, did
she need this. Just as Adam contained a deep need that
he could no longer address himself,[a] so Eve also knew
lack. Newly minted as on the first day of high school, Eve
was like the lonely girl standing mortified in the cafeteria,
holding her tray in those excruciating moments when she
realizes she has nowhere to sit. Adam gives her a place,
telling her that she does belong and how she does belong.
This service that the man provides forms the basis of a
principal act of gender distinction, and what you should
count on in a man: he is there to secure you.

His securing gives you a place for your identity to
be known. It also dispels danger from your life. You can
expect, and ask for, a close man to stand up to the enemies
that threaten you. This derives, understandably, from
the archetype in the triune relations of God. Our earthly,
limited securing somehow mirrors this way of the Promiser, the first Person of the Trinity, so named in the last
chapter, with the Beloved, the second Person of God. One
Scripture describing this dynamic is Psalm 110:1:

> The LORD says to my Lord:
> "Sit at my right hand,
>   until I make your enemies your footstool."

Although this verse does not come up on many Bible
believers' favorite-verses lists, it does seem to be a favorite
in the Holy Writ itself. Appearing no less than six times
in the Bible,[b] used in books of five different authors, this

---

a. Gen 2:18; Gen 2:20.
b. Mat 22:44; Mar 12:36; Luk 20:43; Act 2:35; Heb 1:13. Psalm 110:1 is possibly quoted
   more if Psalm 8:6, which seems to have been written later, is itself based on this

verse is one of the verses of the Bible most quoted by the Bible. Why so many repeats? The answer, I think, is in the scene's import in showing what Christ did and how the triune relationship enabled the doing.

The great King David originally penned these words in a psalm that came to be recognized as a Messianic prophecy.[52] In other words, it is an exchange between God and the Christ. In the Gospels, Jesus then uses this verse to force the question of who He was, identifying Himself as the second "Lord" in the sentence. According to the author of Hebrews, this second Lord bears the imprint of the nature of the First.[a] The apostle Peter likewise identifies this character as the Ascended One Who is securely seated at the Almighty God's right hand.[b] So we are definitely getting the trinitarian Persons here in David's report, and the First Person is doing something for the Second.

In explaining the psalm's words, the author of Hebrews tells how God makes the Christ's Kingdom secure: "Your throne... is forever and ever."[c] Here's the thing. The action of the Almighty Promiser, in Their earthly activity, is to so disperse the forces against the Beloved that the latter Lord comes to a secure place, with feet supported by what were previously threats. Even the Beloved's enemies are made a footstool. Other Scriptures to which we could turn show this same action. For example, when the Christ is about to enter a situation of great vulnerability and God calls out from the sky in

"putting enemies under his feet," as that latter verse is also repeated at least four more times (1Co 15:25, 1Co 15:27; Eph 1:22; Heb 2:8).
a. Heb 1:13 with verse 3.
b. Act 2:33-36.
c. Heb 1:13 with verse 8.

affirmation,[a] or when Christ's soul is sorely troubled, God answers with upholding.[b] In other words, the Promiser secures the Beloved.

Such incarnation-bound interactions do not tell us exactly what goes on among the eternal Persons. The eternal Beloved has no enemies, nor any insecurity, nor any lack at all. But these actions certainly do, and must, give us an analogy of the divine triune life. In the eternal procession, the Second being *of* the First means that the First gives grounding to the personhood of the Second. The Promiser moves for the Beloved as hypostatically generated to know "Her" Self as One eternally loved, without interruption or disruption, forever. This deep trinitarian pattern becomes imprinted on the masculine and feminine and calls forth the securing of a human woman by a human man.

Now, when you are dating you are not there yet, but this image is where you are heading. Shana was the first girl way back when who said yes to dating me (at last!). She was a real beauty. Shana was so beautiful, in fact, that I had a hard time even talking to her. The next day, I passed right by her in the school hallway without talking to her because I couldn't really believe that she had said yes. It didn't take long for her to conclude that this was not going to work. I could not bring her security if she was too high on a pedestal for me to reach. Things ended quickly. Smart girl.

Susan was another dater who understood this well.

a. Mat 3:17–4:1; Mar 1:11–13; Luk 3:22; Luk 4:1–2.
b. Joh 12:27–28.

As a young woman in her twenties, she discovered over time that she was dating an alcoholic. I admired how she tried, but it became clear that Oliver had no plans to change. Although he had a lot of advantages, including great long arms to hold her, she decided that this guy was not going to be able to provide security for her. She broke things off with him and made room for a man who could. She is now abundantly secure in a happy marriage to Benjamin. This second guy has two nice arms to hold her also. It turns out that they are not terribly hard to come by.

In Search of a Dragon Slayer

So, the simple dating question is, how does this guy do in making me secure, in "making my enemies into my footstool?" To answer this dating question well, first ask this question: *What are my enemies? What are those things that make me afraid? Who are those people that take away my peace? What is it that makes me insecure? Then ask yourself: Are there ways I notice that I am made to feel safe in his presence? Do I feel less anxious by the things that he does? Is he willing to address my dragons?*

A godly, masculine dragon slayer does not always go out with a spear on horseback against others. Sometimes your insecurities are founded inside you and he helps you see how no amount of change to your outward conditions will dispel your fears. A good dragon slayer does not always make you feel comfortable. He may surprise you at times, or even make you worry, but he has ways, in the end, that make you confident.

* * *

Before Holly came to adore him, there were some strange things about Lucas that she needed to overcome. One time in college, Lucas left a flower at her dorm room door. It had no note, so she didn't know who it came from. A few days later, he left a flowering twig there, with several flowers on it. Nice, but again no ID. Then came the day when he left a large branch there, which made it difficult to get into the room. He would also randomly sing to different people on campus as if he were in a musical. Like I said, somewhat strange. Not exactly dangerous behavior. Just not entirely reassuring.

What was it that brought Holly to her resolution that, if he asked, she would say yes? Largely two things. The first was how deliberate Lucas was, how careful with his words. At one point she told him to be clear about his intentions toward her. They needed to define the relationship (DTR). After that, he was clear at each stage what he could promise her and what he couldn't. Think back to Jesus Christ with the disciples at the Last Supper: "If it *weren't* true, I would have told you" (chapter 1). Along the way, Lucas's way of speaking, even with others on other matters, secured her. The second assurance was the way he treated his friends, loving them in the mix of their trials and troubles. His patience with them gave her a sense of how she would be treated. These things made her feel safe around him, like her enemies becoming her footstool. Holly decided that she wanted to commit to Lucas for life. In fact, she began hoping and hoping that he would ask.

Sometimes this happens unconsciously, which is great.

The guy just has a way that grounds you. But sometimes it needs an explicit request. A guy may not instinctively know these things about you. In your dating, it is not cheating to tell him: "Hey, it makes me confident and secure when you do this," or "Hey, it makes me insecure when you do that." But whether he does it consciously or unconsciously, recognize that we all need to grow. Discern the difference between a man who is immature but has the raw material for dragon-slaying, and one who is just on a track to nowhere. *Alas*, you sigh, *how can I tell the difference with my guy? Is he hopeless or just young?* It may be hard to tell but take some time to think about it and test it. These things can be learned, and a man who is willing to learn securing is a great catch.

A Kid-Honoring Kind of Guy

There are few things that will make your life secure like the prospering of your children, if you have them. You cannot imagine how strong a connection this is, but the state of your heart will be inviolably tied to their welfare. So put two and two together now and think about how your date will do as a father. Does he have enough respect for the home that it plays into his thinking? Or is he on the path to becoming an absentee dad? Remember Alice from that electric conversation with the college guys? After that disappointing conversation, Alice trained her dating eye for a guy who would be good for the children she expected to eventually have. She couldn't guarantee that a man would raise her children well, but she could at least be on the lookout for signs that he was a kid-honoring kind of guy. These signs can appear when your dating includes group activities with different kinds of people.

Alice was eventually rewarded on a ski trip she took with a church group. There was this guy, Jacob, whom she liked, but she wasn't sure about him. On the trip to the mountain, though, Alice watched Jacob tell a story to one of the younger children in the group, Ava, making it up as he went along. Later, when Ava was struggling on her skis, Jacob, a skier himself, took a good couple of hours of the morning to help Ava out. That was it. Alice started falling in love from that moment. And she really fell. Jacob and Alice eventually did get together, and they have had many happy years together… along with four children. Alice was not disappointed in searching for a man who could make a secure household by handling children.

~ ~ ~

For Men: What Is She Made Of?

Adam, the first guy who bore God's image, had a problem starting out. He was missing something. It seems like he didn't even recognize it at first. He had a good job[a] and a lot of great friends.[b] He ate well.[c] Everything in life seemed terrific.[d] But as time wore on, this privation became apparent. What was it? God called it the want of a "helper fit for him."[e] It is hard to tell all that those words mean. The best place to look is whence the solution came,

---

a. Gen 2:15; Gen 2:19.
b. Gen 2:20.
c. Gen 1:29; Gen 2:16.
d. Gen 1:25; Gen 1:31.
e. Gen 2:18.

which, as we've read, was Adam's own substance. Adam
was in a state of profound rest when Eve was born, and
her genesis ripped him from that respite. But only tempo-
rarily. When he meets his rib again, now in the form of a
woman, his hand probably went to his side with that deep
sigh he made, "At last!"[a]

In the first four words Adam utters, more literally,
"This at-last bone of-my-bones," the second word is פַעַם
(*pa-am*), a noun that means "a time" or "a finality."[53] In
this context, the term hearkens back to preceding events, a
conclusion to something that happened before. Adam
applies the current relief to his bones ("bone of my
bones"). What had just happened to his bones in the
previous two verses?[b] His rib was ripped out of him! Now,
just from her presence, he regains that lost peace, a return
to rest. "At last," he says, looking (across a romantic
clearing in the woods?) at his rest-bringer. He recognized
her as the one to bring a deep peace. Guess what? You are
in this story too. Because you want to find a woman who
does for you what Eve did for Adam. Your individual
peace may come from many graces she brings, a few of
which we explore below: support, acceptance and a home
life. But however that "at last" comes out of you, it will
come of asking of your date: *What is this woman made of?*

Different Beds to Lie In

As you search for a wife, you may have in mind a woman
with whom it will be good to have sex when you are

a. Gen 2:23.
b. Gen 2:21–22.

married. This is fine. But after you marry, God will set
about teaching you the most important thing about sex.
It is this: sex is about a lot more than sex. Attraction is
important. But you had better carefully distinguish the
rest-giving woman from the merely sexy woman. The
two are not the same.

I will never forget Roxanne, a woman in one of the
churches I pastored. She took me by surprise. At the time,
I was spending a lot of time seeking to fortify the women
in my church. It was the women, I thought, who needed
to guard the gold of their bodies against predatory guys.
Therefore, there was a lot of talk about a girl not giving in
to giving the gift of sex outside of a lifelong commitment
from the guy. But pastoring Roxanne, I understood for
the first time how a woman could be the real problem.
Women also, it turns out, have sensual desires that can
lead them and others into sin.[a] Roxanne had a contagious,
vivacious personality. But she was not only a woman who
couldn't say no, she really didn't want to. It became clear
in her confessions during counseling sessions that she was
a seductress. There was enough age difference so that it
was not directed at me, but she was honest with me about
her history and motivations with guys. That it was wrong
she well understood. She was convicted by the Holy
Spirit, as they say, and knew that she needed to change.
But it would be a while before she could have a good
relationship.

There really are these women out there who, for
a variety of reasons, are not interested in love. Unlike

---

a. 1Ti 5:11–12.

Roxanne, they do not wish to change. They will bring you down to a place from which you will be hard pressed to recover.[a] I have met such Delilahs and by God's grace was not entangled. But I can see how easily it could happen.[b] The point is: do not waste your time with such women who cannot and do not want to bring rest. Save yourself like a gazelle from the hunter.[c] Adam discerned it by Eve's presence. One way or another, you can too.

My friend, the talented and handsome Rowan, married the beautiful Brianna on a fateful spring morning. The vivacious bride seemed to have it all. But I wish I could have seen far enough ahead to advise Rowan against the matrimony. At the time he ignored the salient fact that she had dated a married man in college, thinking all that was in the past. One time a pastor gave her the discerning warning against "playing at being a Christian" to no avail. Brianna committed adultery twice on Rowan. They ended up divorced with their family in shambles. My one consolation is that Rowan is now happily remarried—but not without deep scars.

Your Friends Aren't Marrying Her

Another needed caution concerns your friends' role in making the decision about whether this one is the one for you, especially if the assessment of friends dominates your own. What they think of her will give her a high status or low one in your mind. In that movie, *Marty*,

---

a. Pro 2:16–19; Pro 5:3–5; Pro 7:27.
b. Pro 7:5–26.
c. Pro 6:5.

Marty's (Ernest Borgnine) friends had a poor opinion of Clara (Betsy Blair). I believe the term they used was *dog*. Although not a noticeable beauty, it is kind of funny that Blair is called a dog, because in real life she had been married to hunk movie star Gene Kelly for fourteen years.

Certainly, family and friends are valuable for offering perspective on your prospect. You should listen to what they have to say and weigh it, especially your parents. But your brother is not going to be marrying this woman. Your best friend from college is not going to be spending his life with her. They can be wrong. Remember, marriage is a process of *leaving*.[a] Just as Marty had to overcome the opinion of his friends (and mother!) to commit to this girl, so you have to, in the end, stand alone on your decision. The real question is what you think of her, what you have with her, whether she brings *you* rest.

A Good Ribbing

If people were honest, you would hear many stories of doubt before marriage, especially during engagement. No one really wants to admit that he is having doubts, but sometimes it gets unbearable. And then it is inconveniently blurted out in the middle of dinner or while giving the dog a haircut. But commitment reticence is not unusual. We simply have no way to foresee the future and how it will work out. The more realistic the person, the more subject to doubts.

Well that was Lucas. While Holly, from earlier in this

---

a. Gen 2:24.

chapter, was getting past some of Lucas's quirks, he was feeling a deep appreciation for human sinfulness. As he ruminated on the very accurate theological doctrine of our abiding sin—namely, that we are all liable to fall in sin until the day we die, it frightened him. He knew his own failings. He surmised that Holly had hers as well. *How could anyone become successfully married?* Besides that, he was detecting that she and he had some minor theological disagreements. What led Lucas, beset by doubts as he was, to pull the trigger? To not only ask her, but follow through with the whole thing (which he did)? Something happened in Lucas's heart as he spent time with Holly. He came to appreciate, with a deep relief, how she could stick it out with him when he failed. She gave him rest when he faltered. The rest he felt in that drove the decision to go through with it. There was a lot more to come in how Holly created rest for Lucas, but that was the great beginning. Today they are having many happy adventures together as husband and wife.

So, while dating your lady, wonder, *Can she bring me rest?* This was essentially the standard used by the servant of Abraham in locating a wife for his son, Isaac.[a] With no context whatsoever to go on, the servant devised a test— whether a woman would water his camels—to secure a hospitable woman for the son. Could she give rest to him? To wonder well yourself, first ask, *What gives me rest?* (Not what gives your friends rest.) The answer is going to vary with the guy, but that is the question. For Lucas, it became about how she handled his failures, or even

---

a. Gen 24.

sins. Is she able to help you with them to maintain your rest and move toward overcoming them? Girls do this a lot for guys. The magical gift of God-given gender works well when a guy so opens himself up. You might also put it, *What are those things, or people, that take my rest?* In a good mate you find that those things don't matter so much anymore. On a good date, they should start not to. She should give you a hope that they can come to not matter.

'The Wisest of Women Builds Her House'

Another way to frame the rest question is, *What makes a home for me?* Again, the answer will vary with the guy, but you will be greatly helped by a woman with some homebuilding aspirations. So emphasizes the New Testament letter to Titus:

> Older women likewise are to… train the young women to love their husbands and children and to be… home-focused (οἰκουργοὺς, oikourgous) [or working at the home].[a]

Paul uses a specific word, not meaning "to be at home" but "to work at making the home." A central stable hearth is a platform of prosperity for a family. It acts as a base from which the two of you accomplish great things. It gives health to both of you and provides needed stability for children. It is also a waystation for the needy.

---

a. Tiu 2:3–5, author's translation.

Before children come, and after they leave, your house- or apartment-tending effort is less substantial. The basic requisites of a Christian home without children are things like social responsibility, shared worship, and especially hospitality. She should be able to help you welcome those in need and those you disciple. But the need for a wife's focus on the home then may not be as pronounced.

Once children come, the game changes. These days, that change takes many couples by surprise. Most education does not encourage a realistic picture of the future so they are not adequately prepared for actually having a family. Furthermore, housewifery is actively denigrated in many circles. By the way some talk, you would think that to be a home-building woman is to be consigned to a Roman slave ship, only without the stale bread-and-water rations. This distortion leads to an unrealistic view of life and so a failure to prepare for children. Yet still "the wisest of women builds her house."[a]

* * *

Ferdinand and his friend were sitting out on a patio one beautiful evening, as the sun was setting, speaking with Suzanne, a single Yale Law School student. The conversation was free and expansive and eventually happened upon the difficulties of running a household. The guys were respectfully wondering how Suzanne was envisioning handling it, or not, in her life after law school. Suzanne had some options jobwise, but she said that it wouldn't be a problem. She was ready to make any decisions needed based on her priorities.

---

a. Pro 14:1.

"What were those priorities?" the guys asked.

"I believe that the highest calling a person can have is being a wife and mother," Suzanne answered. Ferdinand and his friend nearly fell off their chairs, as that was the last answer they expected from this student of Secretary of State Hillary Clinton's alma mater. Secretary Clinton once derided these callings with the dismissive characterization of being simply about baking cookies.

Ferdinand squinted in the setting darkness to study her face, trying to see if Suzanne was really serious. She was. She went on to elaborate on the glorious impact of these home-building callings, how the stable home has formed the bedrock of any healthy society that ever was, how women in that calling have a unique ability to be the glue that holds many together, how well-raised children can extend the work of a couple and change the world. Suzanne had a well-developed explanation of how motherhood generated culture. Ferdinand was struck, not only by the unabashed esteem he was hearing for home-building, but by the strength of this woman's convictions in the midst of an environment quite hostile to her views. Ferdinand was already focused on another girl, so he did not pursue Suzanne. "But," he later told me, "if I weren't already dating someone else…"

Our information economy and increasing urban dwelling foster many work opportunities for both women and men, which is helpful for couples. And there are seasons of different work-home combinations. And there are even outliers, couples whose mission (and consequent income) are so focused on the woman's work that a stay-at-home dad is the result. With attention and care to the broad biblical principles, these can work (as described in chapter 10), but they are not the norm. Unless you are one of those, you should be looking for a woman who wants to, and can, forge a stable hearth from which the two of you can achieve God's mission. Is your date one of these "wisest of women"?

Can She Delight to be Wisdom?

The Titus 2 passage cited above is not a novelty. Its author is building on Old Testament wisdom, found especially in the book of Proverbs.[a] Why would the book of Proverbs, the royal youth manual (chapter 2), emphasize home-building as a characteristic of the "wisest of women,"[b] as if home-building was rooted deeply in womanhood? Recall that Proverbs is one of those places we are also given a feminine metaphor for the second Member of the Trinity, as seen through God creating the world. The world was made through the Beloved One (whom we know as Christ),[c] but *how* Christ did it shows how women are the image of this divine Person.

When Beloved Christ creates or re-creates, the work is one of making the earth a place of rest for God, or a "footrest" for the Promiser.[d] The only way this refreshment ever comes about on the earth for Him is through the Beloved.[e] When the earth was being created the first

---

a. Pro 11:16; Pro 30:10–31; contra Pro 7:11.
b. Pro 14:1.
c. Joh 1:10; Heb 1:2.
d. Mat 5:35; Act 7:49.
e. Isa 66:1–2. Chapter 8 of this book elaborates.

time as God's footrest in Proverbs 8, the Beloved is there, portrayed as Wisdom personified. Giving this feminine rest was the Woman Wisdom's profound delight. That she could actually give such delight to the Promiser seems to tickle her to no end, as she puts it, "rejoicing before him always."[a] True femininity can delight in the creation of rest. The particulars are not as important as the attitude in the woman you are dating.

Look for this. You may need to discern potential if ability is not yet there. Women have a lot to overcome these days to even recognize the value of giving these things to a man. She might not be ready, but does she want to learn to be a rest-maker? Having these questions on your mind will elevate your dates spiritually and help win you the best girl spirituality can buy.

---

a. Pro 8:30–31.

Six

Can He Take Charge for Us? / Can She Esteem Me?

"Males call some vulnerability out of me, some weakness out of me… call for me to remain like that… [Those relationships were] a giving up of authority, … diminishing both [of us].… Hers was just the opposite: 'No, come forth. Be strong. Be solid. Be real. Be man.'"
— "Silva," a former homosexual man now married to a woman [54]

He who never sacrificed a present to a future good or a personal to a general one can speak of happiness only as the blind do of colors.
— Olympia Brown (allegedly) [55]

In this chapter I am going to tell you, both of you, that you think that you want one thing, but you really want something else. The burden of convincing you of this is one that I hope I can rise to shoulder. Let us start with you, dear woman reader.

For Women: Gender Lack in *La La Land*

The mesmerizing movie, *La La Land*, came out in 2016 and went on to win many awards. It tells a common story.

A young girl travels to the big city to make it (in this case, Los Angeles), has some struggles, begins sleeping with a musician, and then has her heart broken. However, this time the story is told by way of reviving the genre of movie musical in a highly sophisticated and technically stunning manner. Brilliantly staged, Mia (Emma Stone) and Sebastian (Ryan Gosling) float along through the romance. Certain realities are skipped over, though, like how cohabitation outside of marriage will scar you, as we have discussed. The movie works, as the old musicals did, only to the degree that the leads act, or dance, genderly toward one another. Sometimes gender is evoked by the slightest gesture of award-deserving Emma Stone.

There is an apparent dilemma for this couple cohering as they pursue their careers. They split up, but the reason is mystifying. Why is there any problem with them staying together when Mia goes off to film a movie in Paris? With the kind of money Sebastian now has, and Mia will soon be making, why couldn't he fly to France for a monthly weekend? Haven't they heard of the internet? There is no discernible reason for these two, who seem custom-made for each other, to cut off the relationship. But they do. Why? Because there has been no commitment made to hold them together.

Who should have made that commitment? Who should have taken that step of faith in their relationship? We can pinpoint the big moment of gender failure in the film. On a park bench, Mia looks to Sebastian for direction.

"Where are we?" she asks, speaking of the relationship. Being a modern man, and so feeling no responsibility to take charge and clarify, he makes a joke instead.

"We're on a park bench."

"No," she insists, "Where *are* we?"

Then he answers, "I don't know."

She tries again: "So what are we going to do now?"

He doesn't know that either, and this is the modern part. Sebastian feels no responsibility to pursue her. He feels no gendered obligation, even after taking her affections, taking her body, taking her first faith in love. Consequently, they part and each loses the love of their lives. They lose that which would have made their great careers worth it. End of movie. Maybe that is why, at the 2017 Academy Awards, she won best actress, but he lost as best actor. Instead, it went to Casey Affleck, who spent his time in his winning movie getting into fights with guys. When you lose gender, you lose.

Remember how upset Rebekah got in real life with Troy's post in chapter 2? He similarly was not seeing a need to step forward for them, but unlike Mia with Sebastian, real-life Rebekah called Troy on it. The episode led to a very helpful argument about what was appropriate posting and what each could expect at this stage of the relationship. Rebekah's impulse of jealousy was not inappropriate. It was the good kind. It was about whether Troy was going to take ownership for their relationship. Sebastian and Troy and many men do not. Men not taking initiative in dating is one big symptom of the modern destruction of gender. Real-life Rebekah eventually broke up with real-life Troy over just this lack.

Finding a Firstborn

I suppose we should back up and speak about what you want. Maybe you have not thought about it this way, but you want a man in whom you can invest authority. In other words, you want a guy who is able to take charge for you. Those last two words are important. Maybe you have experienced men taking charge selfishly. So, it may not seem to you now like you will want charge-taking in a guy. But you will. As we've noted, God did not make Adam and Eve at the same time, but in a different order,[a] and that makes a difference in how their sons and daughters love each other.[b]

How does that matter in your dating? The first is in the asking itself. A man taking charge is first expressed in overcoming the terror in asking you out. If you haven't realized this yet, it is a terrifying thing for him, even if you have made signs that you like him. You may feel as if you have practically rolled out a red carpet sided with golden rope stanchions inviting him to approach you, and painted hearts all over your forehead beckoning him to ask you, but he still does not see it. You may feel like you have broadcast your openness with loudspeakers set to eleven, mounted on a flamboyant float parading around him for months, but he remains oblivious, like Snoopy lying face up on top of his doghouse. That may be because he just is not interested in you. But it may also be because what he hears is that persistent doubt inside: that, if you really knew him, you couldn't want him. And he has yet to learn

---

a. 1Ti 2:13.
b. 1Ti 2:12.

the love of God to overcome it. You must wait for him to learn it.

Women need to be very careful here. The third-wave feminism that tries to establish that there is no difference between men and women does not help you. If you convince men that they are no different from women, they will stop asking you out on dates. And if you think that you will just ask him out instead, you are stunting his growth. He will learn from your innocent act that he does not have to become a man. And that will plague your relationship for a long, long time.

* * *

Patty had recently converted to Christianity and was earnestly trying to submit herself to God. She didn't know how this Christianity thing worked and was looking to others to find out. She and Boris were certainly friends, being in the same church. She had had some pleasant exchanges with him, but she wasn't prepared for what came next. They were sitting on a hill. The air was charged. Boris paused, took a deep breath, and finally got it out. He asked her, "Has God told you that we should be married?" Patty caught her breath and fumbled for an answer, something like "No… why?" She spent the rest of the conversation trying to make things less awkward for him.

Boris and Patty's exchange, unfortunately not unique, demonstrates a particularly religious way of a man avoiding responsibility. Boris put the cherry on top by not even phrasing it as "God told me… " but rather making it into a question for Patty about what God might have told her. Without getting into the question of how God usually directs us, let's just say, for the sake of argument, that a guy did somehow receive this privileged information about your future; the veil was pulled back revealing a vision of him being with you. What should he do with that information? Well, when people in the Bible received privileged information from God that affected the destiny of unwitting loved ones, they did much better by being quiet about it. Young Joseph, son of Jacob, upon being shown his future as a supreme ruler, made a mess of his life by reciting his dreams to his brothers.[a] On the other hand, David, being anointed as king while the current king Saul remained in power, patiently sat on the information through many excruciating years before obtaining the crown.[b] Mary, witness to extraordinary prophecies about her baby son Jesus, did not call the *Jerusalem Times* to spread the word. She wisely chose to "treasure these things up in her heart."[c] Boris would have gotten much farther with Patty if he had just told her that he liked her a whole lot.

Citing a dream or vision to ask a girl out—or worse, to propose—wreaks havoc because it shifts the responsibility for the request off of him onto God. Maybe it is God's plan, but you, as a woman, need to know that it is the guy's plan also. That is what it means to be firstborn. This is the first sign you can use to judge if this man is going to be able to carry the authority in your marriage to make it work.

Patty did not get together with Boris. She ended up with Steve, who handled responsibility in the relationship quite differently. She came to appreciate and love that after

a. Gen 37:2–11; Gen 37:19–20.
b. 1Sa 16:13—2Sa 5:3.
c. Luk 2:8–39.

a while. Today she is teaching her three grown children that God uses all of who we are to make decisions like these. We are made with wills specifically because God has a will. Responsibility comes along with having a will. Find someone who can ask you out. Again, Adam was first-born in relation to Eve. Being firstborn means a position of authority[a] for the flourishing of the woman. Does the guy you are dating have any sense of this? Can you see him step forward in situations for you? If he can, is it a matter of his own pride or a matter of your benefit?

Eventually, you should ask: *Can he defy me?* The time to see is that awful moment when you sense that you actually might disagree with one another. There's a heart-break there as your dreams of perfect unity come crashing down all around you. It is okay; it really is. You are two limited creatures, and sinners to boot. But you can still have a wonderful life together, even if you do not agree on everything. The important thing in that moment is how you both handle the disagreement. What happens when you defy him? Can he hold to his convictions without caving to you? Let's say that you are discussing a decision he is making about his life that doesn't concern you and, after you have talked about it thoroughly and you still disagree, can he stick to his course of action?

Rooting for a Representative

Sometimes people wonder why there are no women priests in the Bible. There are priestesses aplenty in other

---

a. Some examples showing this meaning are Psalm 89:27, Colossians 1:15–18, and 1 Timothy 2:12–13.

ancient cultures and religions, but not in Israel. Israelite
prophetesses pop up from time to time, but no feminine cultic vestments ever.⁵⁶ Why might this be? Priests
were there to be present with the people, helping them
in their spiritual walk. When things worked right and
the priests were doing their job, one can imagine a good
deal of counseling coming from them, as people brought
their sacrifices and their problems to the tabernacle, and
later, the temple. Priests needed sensitive wisdom as they
brought the law to bear on the life knots into which God's
people tend to often get tied. Priests also prayed for the
people as they burnt their sacrifices for them. Whereas the
king ruled for them and protected them, he was necessarily distant. And the prophet came from the divine
throne room, advising the people, but largely the king,
as to God's will according to past promises, the current
covenant, and future hopes. But the priest was there to
intercede for the holy subjects, to bring much-needed
petition before God for them and to rejoice with them in
the answers the Lord would grant in a regular way.

One would think a woman could be quite good at
many of these things, even better than many men. So why
not women priests? Why wouldn't God use the fairest of
all creation, "the last and best of all His works" for these
needed tasks for the community? The answer lies in the one
priestly function that was the most important thing that
a priest did, the *sine qua non* of priestly-ness: representation.

The priest was there to represent the people to God,
and to represent God to the people. Representing was the
priest's *raison d'etre*. And that foundational function was

established for man in close relationship, so men could become men. As Adam was formed to represent Eve and the rest of the human family to God, in their creation[a] and in their sin,[b] as a husband is likewise called to represent his wife in their dealings,[c] as men in a church are to especially represent the church family in intercession,[d] and as Christ the Bridegroom will be the church's "priest forever,"[e] so God arranges His people to encourage men to this masculine feature. Christ deeply fulfilled that representation for His bride when He became, not only our priest, but the very sacrifice as well,[f] offered on the cross on our behalf.

Sacrificial representing is essential for manliness, so you should be looking for it in a man. Can you see your guy willing to step forward in appropriate moments to represent the close women in his life? Rather than hanging back to see how it turns out, can he stand up when no one else wants to and take the lead to resolve the issue? Instead of making sure the appropriate party in your family feels the blame for some wrong, could he assume the priesthood for your family and make sacrifice for them? Christ, our model husband, did just this for us, His bride. He owned the responsibility for our sin. Can your guy go to God for the family and accept for the sin, not necessarily the blame, but the responsibility?

Madison is a straightforward woman who has already been through a marriage and a difficult but righteous

---

a. E.g., in Genesis 5:3 and First Chronicles 1:1, of Eve and Adam, Adam is assigned the passing on of the image.
b. Gen 3:9; Rom 5:12-21.
c. E.g., Gen 3:9; Joh 4:15-16.
d. E.g., 1Ti 2:8.
e. Psa 110:4.
f. Heb 7:26-27; Heb 9:12.

divorce. (Both Jesus and Paul, in the New Testament, acknowledge that certain conditions can make divorce a sadly unavoidable but good thing to do.[a]) As she speaks about how she is handling her dates now, I can only listen with admiration. She recently queried Ethan, a guy she was engaging with online, "What is the most recent sin that you have repented of?" Ethan had to think back a few years. Madison was not impressed and began to lose interest. She thought, "Is this man going to be a fit representative to lead us in repentance when we need it?"

So another way to ask the question of the firstborn is: *Do I want this guy as a representative? Maybe he can take charge, but is he capable of being a trusted authority in my life?* Some husbands can wield authority aplenty, but it is not for their wives' flourishing. *Is he a guy I want to submit to because he merits my submission?* If the answer is no, it is better to end it now. Escape like a bird from a fowler.[b] A woman has a right to let her heart ask these questions.

As time goes on, that representation becomes ever more important. When we read the accounts of the early life of the Messiah, the stars of the show, of course, are Jesus and Mary. But if we examine how the holy family functions, the family of this "righteous man," Joseph,[c] we find God honoring this masculine representation to guide them through the most dangerous periods of the vulnerable family's life. It was specifically to Joseph, the family's representative, that God gives direction for their survival.[d]

---

a. Mat 1:19; Mat 19:9; 1Co 7:10–15.
b. Pro 6:5.
c. Mat 1:19 (NIVO).
d. Mat 1:19–24; Mat 2:13–15; Mat 2:19–23; Luk 2:1–5.

This firstborn stuff matters to you and your date for these reasons. One day, you will probably have a baby. You want a man who can assume authority for the flourishing of your children. Your job raising your kids will be tons easier if your husband can act as a head for them.[a] This might not be what you are thinking on a date, but try to look ahead. Look to see if he can assume some caring authority for the date.

To find a guy on this track is not to say that he is yet worthy of full admiration. Our dates rarely show up like the Star Wars Death Star, "fully functional" and able to destroy any planetary power at will. But is the potential there at least? Is he heading in the right direction? Does he know where he is heading? Can you squint your eyes and see the man he is becoming?

~ ~ ~

For Men: Sex is about More Than Sex

Like many women who do not realize what they actually want, you as a man may not either. I would like you to have great physical intimacy in your life. But the great enemy of our souls, in common parlance, the devil—yes, he is still around[b]—has a program of reduction. As Satan hates the fullness of blessing in God's creation, he is out to thwart it for people. He cannot stand the way that God's gifts bring wholeness and praise to us, so he struggles to do away with them in our world. He cannot abolish them,

a. Col 3:21; Eph 6:4.
b. 1Pe 5:8.

because the pleasures of the creation are so resilient. The best he can do is reduce their dimensions with people, to cheapen their joy and diminish their benefit to us. On account of his work, the many blessings God has built into our lives are reduced to so much less than they are meant to be. So eating is reduced to just consumption, travel to just a commute, family to just "an arrangement," worship to just entering the praise zone, and, yes, lovemaking to just sex.

It turns out, by any measure since the 1960s sexual revolution, married folks have the best sex.[17] Why would this be? It is because healthful, covenant-confirming lovemaking glues two people together and propels them to full-bodied intimacy. The world's program for sex would coax you to the fantasy that sex is simply about meeting a physical desire that is unrestrained by commit-ment, unloaded with wisdom about God, and unrelated to God's purposes for you in marriage. In this view, sex loses the very mystery the Bible says that it should have.[a] Buying into the world's program for sex is one of the worst decisions you can make about your life.

As we saw in chapter 2, sex is not just about sex. What makes for good sex over the long-term is the relationship it is meant to support and develop. A physical climax is a psycho-spiritual-somatic event that depends upon many other factors besides physical characteristics of the partner. The thoughts that you are able to have during the love-making determine the quality of the climax event. All this is to say that, as a guy, you should not just go for the best measurements and the prettiest face.

---

a. Pro 30:18–19.

The battle of your life is a battle against covetousness. When you recognize how many things there are to enjoy in the wife before you whom God has made, it helps to deliver you from having to have *every* gift that God has made. There are many more ways to sexual arousal than you suppose. But you must be able to explore them in a marriage. Covetousness, fueled by pornography and other forms of Satanic reduction, kills that exploration.

* * *

Connor could hardly believe that he had arrived at his honeymoon. He had had moments of wondering whether he would ever be married, especially as a man who had through his whole life experienced strong same-sex attraction. Yet today he had just married the lovely younger Violet and it had been a tremendous day. Now he was anxious about what would come next. Like many guys with same-sex attraction who go on to marry women, he worried if he could have a good physical relationship with his new wife. As Connor put it rather pointedly to me, he worried whether the past would kill the future.

It didn't. It turned out that Connor's father died just before the wedding, and he spent a lot of the honeymoon crying. He was, of course, happy to finally be with Violet, but he just missed his dad. Violet swung into action, being patient, being his comfort, being close. She set out to promote him as her husband. With each passing day, as they drew close through her honor of him, he grew in awe and wonder at the beauty of her body. He experienced the thrill of this woman giving herself to him and only to him. Sex was a matter of esteem.

Not all of us start from Connor's place of disadvantage in approaching a woman, but the dynamics of encountering the glory of the female body, through the relationship of honor, will be the same for you. Connor now says that marriage, beginning there in that honeymoon, helped him embrace his masculinity as nothing else ever has. You would be wise to likewise look for the qualities that make for true womanliness. You will have great sex.

A Supernatural Sign That We Were Meant to Be Together

When I met my wife, Mary K., she was a great contrast to my sisters. My three older sisters did not afford me very much respect, most likely because first, they were older sisters, and second, because I deserved little of it. Mary K., on the other hand, had a desire, from the very beginning, to esteem me. She was actually trying to see if she could respect me. This was a marvel to me. Here was this woman, getting close to me, who still wished to promote me. This wonder was instrumental in us coming together.

Things worked out easily for us. Mary K.'s desire to see if I could lead made it seem like things came easy. At the time, I immaturely attributed this sensation to a supernatural occurrence that signified that we should be together: Things always worked out well when we were together. It was a sign! I related this conviction to Mary K.'s friend, Brooklyn, who was a no-nonsense kind of gal. She dryly observed that our ease of operation was

more due to a feature of Mary K. than a cosmic conver-
gence of the planets. Brooklyn was right. I simply had a
girl in front of me who wanted to see me step forward in
authority. That made all the difference. But, in the end, it
was supernatural. To have two equal people, a woman and
a man, both made in the image of God, with one surren-
dering prerogative to the other, is something from another
world. It is so unusual and unlikely a setup, that the
apostle Paul must look to the heavens for its origin. And
he finds it in an order in the divine Persons, where the first
Member of the Trinity, the Promiser, became head to the
Beloved Second[a] (as noted above in chapter 4). Thus, for it
to do what it does in a human relationship *is* a supernatural sign. I think I was right after all.

When Paul says "the head of a wife is her husband,
and the head of Christ is God" he could be speaking of
Christ in His state of becoming a limited human being,
submitting as Redeemer in the plan of salvation. But this
drives us to the question of why the second Member of the
Trinity took on that submission in the first place. The order
of the First sending the Second is never reversed in any of
God's acts, revealing how it would not be fitting that the
Promiser be sent and it is most fitting that the Beloved was.
There is something of an appropriate disposition in the love
of the Beloved, though equal, to step forward to be sent.
That sending became a life here of promoting the Prom-
iser to take charge for the benefit of the Beloved. Sooner
or later, as we trace back the reason for God sending
Christ, we end up in the procession of the Beloved from

---

a. 1Co 11:3.

the Promiser, the One's eternal begetting of the Other, of which, according to Paul, marital headship among us is an analogy. Arising from Their eternal relation of generation, the Second promotes the First. The trinitarian, messianic prophecy of Psalm 22 reveals a heart in the Redeemer to "tell of your name to my brothers; in the midst of the congregation I will praise you."[a] Christ found purpose in doing that,[b] promoting God by praise at every turn.[58] Paul's point is that a feature of womanhood mirrors this.

While we, as boyfriends, should not be praised as God is, the image in gender is promotion, an active practice of submission. The scriptural gender norms for the image of God testify to this femininity in relationship. The same Word that proclaims women and men as equal in Genesis 1[c] also makes an order among them toward each other in Genesis 2.[d] God gave us both Genesis 1 and Genesis 2 to properly see ourselves. The New Testament elucidates the same principle of asymmetry.[e] Can your date embrace this attitude? Can you see in her the heavenly pattern and the Genesis double-truth of how a woman loves a man?

Laboring Against the Tide

What I am writing here is, of course, not very popular. But cultural resistance to this wisdom is not entirely new.

---

a. Psa 22:22.
b. Joh 12:28; 17:1.
c. Gen 1:27.
d. Gen 2:18-23.
e. The explicit passages are Mark 10:2-12; Matthew 19:3-12; 1 Corinthians 11:1-16; 1 Corinthians 14:33-38; Ephesians 5:22-33; Colossians 3:18-19; 1 Timothy 2:8-15; 1 Timothy 3:1-15; Titus 2:1-8; and 1 Peter 3:1-7.

Paul's exposition of these principles to the ancient Corinthian church twice anticipates contradiction of them.[a] The
problem has plagued us since we began hiding behind
fig leaves.[b] Yet the great vehemence against this counsel
these days is one of the symptoms of the severe breakdown between men and women in our times. Because of
this devastation, young women might initially reject this
teaching but later change their minds as they realize its
wisdom. You should look for a woman who has at least
come to a point of not being ideologically opposed to
biblical asymmetry in love. Some guys are willing to intuit
from their dates' behavior that they will actually practice
submission, even if they won't verbally ascribe to the doctrine. In this case, her actions might prove more promising
than her rhetoric, but counting on such a hope is risky. It
is true that sometimes people don't do what they say they
believe. But it makes it hard if you are trying to look to
the future and decide if you can build a life together.

Plus, the asymmetry of order does not mean that
you should expect a woman to promote you right off the
bat. The great gift of submission should come from her to
you only with time and trust. This means that you are not
looking for a pushover. Rather, you should be looking for
a woman who is looking for a man that she can so respect.
The best woman is one who brings her opinions to the
table. She is not shy in offering her judgments, especially
on matters of righteousness. So, as you go on in dating,
and share more, observe how you come to make decisions
together. Does she engage fully on matters concerning

a. 1Co 11:16; 1Co 14:36–37.
b. Gen 3:16.

you both? Is she ever able to actually yield on instances where you disagree? A man has a right to ask these questions.

Look carefully. You have to try to discern what is the residual polemic of growing up as a daughter of this era and what is truly an inability to submit to righteous, caring leadership. Can you see signs that she wants it? Or does she really not want it? Is there abuse in your girl's past that has left her unable to trust any man? Then you must come to terms with her need for a particular gentleness. Let your heart query.

Can She Give Me Weight?

On the positive side, Paul expresses the asymmetry of order as a wife giving a husband glory (δόξα or *doxa*) in a unique way. "Woman is the glory of man," recalls the Genesis creational distinction of male and female.[a] The Old Testament Hebrew word which Paul's term translates is the Hebrew (כָּבוֹד or *kabohd*). The ideas in this Hebrew term for *glory*, include beauty, majesty and splendor, but the root of the word is "weight." Christ is the glory of God,[b] giving Him weight in our eyes.[59] As the Beloved is the glory of the Promiser, a woman gives weight to the man with whom she is in relationship. You can ask as you date whether this woman can give you that weight in her life.

Before he married, Dylan had chatted with around thirty potential dates online, went on a date with ten or

---

a. 1Co 11:7.
b. Heb 1:3.

fifteen, and reached the dating stage with three different girls. He was deliberate and conscientious in his search. He dated Rose for a year. It was getting pretty serious, he thought. Then Rose moved an hour further away from him to pursue her career. She said that the relationship was important to her—but, Dylan surmised, not that important. This was a final detail on top of others that finally brought Dylan to see that Rose was not going to give him weight. It was a hard break up. But not so hard now, as he has a magnificent marriage with Marigold, who herself is quite busy with an influential career, but who is also very clear on the priority of their relationship and their newborn. They remind me of the words of Solomon: "An excellent wife is the crown of her husband."[a] You should look for a woman with this same heart. It will be a supernatural sign.

~ ~ ~

For Both: Where Have All the Flowers Gone?

This is going to be a hard one. As you, both woman and man, have read this chapter, you may have felt the difficulty of finding such directing men and promoting women in our age of gender minimization. Because boys do not grow up being encouraged to take responsibility for others, fewer know what it really means to care for a woman. As women grow up hearing submission as a dirty word in their relationship vocabulary, fewer still know

---

a. Pro 12:4.

how to promote the close men in their lives. Instead, the equality of the genders (a good and true thing) is emphasized to the point of silencing the calls for boyfriends to lead and for girlfriends to esteem. It is one of the sad features of modern life and the reason it can be hard to know if "this one is the one."

But you should still look. One time, the biblical story finds the prophet Elijah pining away at the top of Mt. Carmel, feeling like he is the only one left with a vision of God's good ways. God has to contradict him. The Lord comes and tells Elijah to get up and get moving. Despite what it feels like, the Lord insists, He has left seven thousand in Israel, who have not bowed the knee to Baal or kissed him.[a] Seven thousand! There were plenty still who didn't buy into Baal's despicable and degrading program. Likewise, God has women who are strong enough to look at the culture's belittling of gender and laugh. There are men of conviction out there who are carrying on with God's counsel and shrugging off the shenanigans of relational wreckage. If you seek for such men, such women—and you may have to seek— you can find them.

---

a. 1Ki 19:15–18.

Seven

Does He Have the Mission for Us? / Can She Empower Our Journey?

I reflect on my reflection and I ask myself the question
What's the right direction to go, I don't know...
Am I a Muppet or am I a man? If I'm a man,
that makes me
a Muppet of a man.
— Gary[60]

"Begone, foul dwimmerlaik, lord of carrion!
Leave the dead in peace!"
A cold voice answered: "Come not between the Nazgul
and his prey! Or he will not slay thee in thy turn. He will
bear thee away to the houses of lamentation, beyond all
darkness, where thy flesh shall be devoured, and thy
shriveled mind be left naked to the Lidless Eye."
A sword rang as it was drawn.
"Do what you will; but I will
hinder it, if I may."
"Hinder me? Thou fool. No living man may hinder me!"
Then Merry heard of all sounds in that hour the strangest.
It seemed that Dernhelm laughed, and the clear voice was
like the ring of steel.
"But no living man am I!"
— The Princess Eowyn[61]

The Great Dispeller of Independence

Humanity has a mission. The Almighty has a purpose for you. The first Chapter of the first book in the Bible lays out the commission:[a] to take charge over the earth to royally develop it and its creatures. God made His powerful images to further His kingdom over all the world. Thousands of years later, Jesus Christ, in a very similar passage, commissions His followers. He repeats that purpose with deeper meaning: to further God's Kingdom all over the world through making disciples.[b]

God created the union of men and women for that purpose also. There is a mission for marriage. The first union was not just to create bliss for the man and woman, although it would. It was also to further the purposes of God's Kingdom on earth. In the second creation story of Genesis, where gender is distinguished, how the first two people will carry out the mission is distinguished too. The man is specifically made to begin the mission, finding his place in the garden and tilling the soil.[c] He then also finds himself with the task of taking intellectual dominion.[d] Woman is made as a strong, divinely empowered help to those same purposes.[e] Something of that dynamic holds for all the children of our first parents, an asymmetry of intent as Paul draws it.[f] As the children of Adam and Eve, when you become one flesh, you bring your purposeful

---

a. Gen 1:26–28.
b. Mat 28:16–18.
c. Gen 2:15.
d. Gen 2:19–20.
e. Gen 2:18.
f. 1Co 11:9.

lives together to make each much more powerful in the mission than you could be alone.

In the process, the arrangement fosters intimacy and contradicts our tendencies to independence. We all eventually need to learn that life is not about doing our own thing. The sooner we can learn this, the better for us. This is why God gives us intergendered relationships. They banish independence in us as we grow to embody the trinitarian Image.

A recent *Wall Street Journal* article titled "When You Can't Stop Competing With Your Spouse"[62] attempts to help marriages with a rivalry problem: "Couples are supposed to operate as a team, but sometimes they compete instead. It's often a sign of envy, which can fester and create resentments." The article, ignoring the deep issues at play like failure at transcendent mission, failure of gender, and failure of virtue, is unable to say anything particularly meaningful. The author leaves us with no better solution than: "They [should] each focus on what they are good at and work as a team." Advice like this will not help any marriage to mature.

Folks today think that matrimonial envy and strife will lessen if you each are left to pursue your own dreams, with the other supporting you in just doing your own thing. That may temper envy, but does not address what inspires the envy in the first place. And that independence leads to, years later, a distant marriage. The couple will have failed to embrace the strategy of the union. God has a different answer to eradicating competition in couples. His method is two-fold. First, He creates gender, drawing a distinction that creates complements and not competitors. We will look at this more closely in chapter 10. Then He takes our attention off our self-promotion by directing us together to His promotion, a bigger job than either of our pursuits.

We wedded folks mostly lower our sights on this matter. We settle for a sub-prime purpose for our marriages—namely, being happy, which makes the matrimony much less than it can be and much weaker than it should be. If we raise our eyes, even briefly, above making the marriage about our own happiness, we tend to settle on the somewhat higher, but not high enough, goals of a career or the family. One of the first steps to dating well is to recognize that God's mission for your relationship is not the man's (or the woman's) career. Nor is it your new nuclear family. It often includes these, but it is not equal to them.

~ ~ ~

For Women: Meeting a Man with a Mission

The beginning of wisdom is fear of the Lord.[a] You cannot go on this kingdom mission with someone who doesn't have at least a Christian confession. Thus, the Bible tells Christians to only marry "in the Lord."[b] This means only dating such.

You need to ask this kind of serious question early on. Valerie, visiting from Sweden, met Jose at a bar, where he was bouncing. She was a nice Christian girl who was on adventure in America through a work visa. She had a good

---

a. Pro 9:10.
b. 1Co 7:39. This follows the Old Testament pattern as in, e.g., Ezra 10.

job here and Jose just seemed like a nice guy. She didn't really want to think things through. She just thought that it would all work out. They spent years together. After the relationship really reached a point of no return, she tried to bring him to church. It ended in a disaster, with Valerie breaking Jose's heart and leaving her fairly traumatized. Valerie made everyone involved learn a hard lesson: dating has a life direction to it.

The question you can and should answer early in your dating is: *Does he have a desire for God's mission? Does he have some kind of spiritual orientation? Is he concerned at all with Christ's concerns?*

Can you explore that question between the theater visits and the tennis matches? I guess I do need to say this: Beware trying to make your date a Christian if he is not. You might think that, as the man you are attracted to is an all-around wonderful guy, he will surely become a believer when he sees how great Jesus Christ is and how much He means to you. There are exceptions where such an initial arrangement works out, but it would not be wise to bank on it.

Restricting your dating to Christians might make you shudder as you survey the playing field. You may feel like your options are limited enough. Such a constraint just destroys any possibility of you getting married. But if you insist on this constraint, because it is so fundamental to what marriage is about, God will seriously back you up.

* * *

Leigh, a graduate student, was young in many ways but had this straight at least. She firmly settled on a wise

course: she would only date guys who have a heart for
Christ. This was tested a few times, once particularly
when she was working on an intense summer program in
the Middle East. She was on a team involved in an archae-
ological excavation, which required these students to work
long hours together in close quarters. Not surprisingly, as
they worked every day together, Jerry developed strong
feelings for Leigh. Very strong. In fact, his persistent
pursuit of her affections became apparent to everyone. But
he was not a Christian and, despite Leigh's conversation
about it and attractive manner of life, he was only interested in considering Leigh, not Christ. It didn't help that
all their friends praised him to her. Over and over Leigh
heard what a great guy Jerry was. Indeed, she could see
for herself his many admirable qualities. Jerry told all his
friends that he had met the woman that he would marry.
He even called his father about it. Finally, to deter his
advances, Leigh just came right out and told him that her
faith in Christ was the most important thing in the world
to her. She couldn't even consider a romantic relationship
with a guy who wasn't heading in that direction.

You would expect this to cool the air between them.
However, after a few weeks he asked her to go for a walk.
As they walked along the beach, Jerry told Leigh that he
had become a Christian. Once she recovered from her
shock, Leigh was overjoyed for him, and marveled at how
God could work in peoples' lives. *It is a wonder how He
moves any of our hearts,* she reflected, as she looked out
over the unrelenting waves breaking on the shore. As Jerry
shared his thoughts and questions with her, she asked if
she could pray for him, right there on the beach. Jerry was

a little taken aback but assented. As she placed her hand on his shoulder and began to pray, Jerry got a pained expression on his face. Then he dropped to his knees and clasped his chest. He was enduring a great pounding sensation, as if he was being struck in the rib cage. "What are you, some kind of witch?" Jerry demanded of her. Leigh was understandably stunned. While she stood there wondering how to respond, Jerry, now visibly frightened, gasped, "I have to confess something to you. I was lying when I said that I became a Christian!" He explained that he really just wanted to date her and thought that this was the way to do it. But his physical reaction when she started to pray literally brought him to his knees over his insincerity.

So there ended the story of Jerry and Leigh. Strangely, even after this rather striking sign, Jerry did not connect the dots of his experience. Despite his fear over what had happened, he still chose not to pursue what it meant or to re-assess the claims of Christ. But Jerry did keep his distance after that. As I say, God will back you up if you are serious about His purposes for your relationship.

Some Simple Mission-Leading Signs

There are ways dating can help you answer the bigger question with littler questions. Even if he is a Christian, is he reading the Bible in any kind of regular way? Can you tell? It is not about book smarts. He doesn't even have to have a head for reading. But one has to read the Scriptures to be applying them.

Then there is the dating itself. Can he take the lead on a date? Can he ever be the one to know where you are going, choose what you are doing? Or are you always the one to set things up, always the travel guide? If so, that should raise further questions in your mind. There are much bigger matters to come, and you need to know now if he will be able to lead the two of you in mission. Is he a Muppet or a man?

Some further questions along these lines concern a life mission. Does your date have a desire for God's work in his vocation and alongside of it? Serving Christ does not only mean vocational ministry, but striving for God's purposes in whatever work or avocation we choose to do. Does he have any sense of this mission at all? Or is he holding back parts of his life from whatever the Lord would want?

* * *

Theresa decided in college to only consider a guy who would hold back nothing in His life from the Lord. She pursued this line of thinking with Horace, a guy with whom she was getting serious. Horace seemed like just such a great catch: student body president, life of the party, a great sense of humor, and the guy was spiritually zealous. They went together to a solid church. In fact, he was heading to seminary to become a pastor and they talked passionately about theology. These qualities helped them overcome some long-distance stretches in their relationship (spanning California and Texas). And what iced the cake was his energy for writing poetry, which he used to gush over Theresa. It was no surprise that when Horace at last asked Theresa to marry him (after first securing her father's blessing), the answer was a definite yes and they were engaged. What could possibly be wrong here?

At one point, as they thought together about their future, a missions opportunity came up and Horace mentioned casually, "I would never be a missionary." Now, this statement could mean different things. It could be a mature man's assessment of his gifts, meaning that he was willing to do what God wanted him to, but he had learned that he would be more effective doing something else. But the sentence could also mean, "Serving God in such a life-upsetting way is not on the table. I wouldn't accept that from God." In further conversation, Theresa found that Horace was really saying the latter. Again, God calls people to many different jobs and vocational ministry or missionary work is not the only work of God. But Horace believed that he knew that God would never ask such a thing of him because it could lead to a life of financial uncertainty. He was basically insisting that he would only accept a comfortable living from God. That fateful remark led to far more earnest conversation and, in six months, the unraveling of the relationship. Theresa realized, painfully, that the man before her was not what he had seemed.

Does Horace's remark seem like a slight thing to you? It wasn't. You and your partner are going to change in many ways over the coming decades. If you step into a union now where you can clearly see a part of his life that he will not surrender to God, then there are likely other parts that will come up with time upon which you will see him also refuse God's hand. That is a serious liability to your marriage's happiness. If you do not want to find yourself with such a partner in ten years, do not marry him now. As my sister once quipped to my daughter, "Go find a man worth submitting to because he has learned to submit to God." As it turns out, Horace quit seminary a few years later and joined a cult in California. Good save, Theresa.

How is your date addressing problems in his life? Hopefully, at some point in the relationship, he will disclose to you what is his relationship to pornography. The breakdown in gender has made porn ubiquitous. I would like to tell you that most Christian guys you will date do not use porn, but sadly I can't. According to the Barna Group,[63] over half of Christian boys over the age of thirteen (and one-third of women) use pornography at least once a month. The statistics do not improve as the boys get older. You might find it disturbing, and demeaning, and you should. Porn and masturbation destroy a man's spirituality and insult his partner or partner to be. If you need any convincing of the harms of pornography use, just consider how divorce rates double when people start watching it. In fact, the brain of a person using porn actually shrinks.[64] Its prevalence is part and parcel of the sad state of the American church today.

But all is not lost. Christ's redemption reaches to all our failings. And sooner or later, you will have to deal with each other's sins. So, wrong as it is, a past with porn provides another testing ground of leadership early on. The main question is: Has he been taking the needed steps of repentance, letting others know and getting help for himself through the church? If he has not, that lack of address is reason to forego a relationship with him. Escape like a bird from the hand of the fowler.[a]

Decisions for Down the Road

These are some simple signs of leadership in a man. They can help you try to answer the big question: *Can this one seek out God's mission for us? Can he lead us in Christ?* That "us" will grow with time because of the fruitfulness of trinitarian love. If you have a family, the spiritual welfare of your children will directly depend on whether they see a mission in the love between their parents.

Remember Leigh? We left her overseas with Jerry now keeping his distance. When she returned to the States, she got set up by some mutual friends with James, a nonbelieving drinker who nonetheless liked to think things through. When he got the same line from Leigh that Jerry got—how Christ is worth putting in front of anything else—he was similarly annoyed. But James had just reached the point of being fed up with living by his stepfather's credo that life is a cruel joke. He had always wanted to pursue spirituality with someone. He found that someone in Leigh. He went, on his own, to investigate Christianity himself, starting with one of the most influential Christians who has ever lived, Augustine, the ancient bishop of Hippo. His reading convicted James of his sin, and he repented and believed in Christ. They

---

a. Pro 6:5.

married and he became a pastor. They are now happily raising a son together, getting him ready to date.

What was the difference between Jerry and James? One was a man with a mission, a man who could recognize God's call on him. So, he was fit to be a husband, to recognize a call on *them.* The other, even with all his great traits, was just a Muppet.

~ ~ ~

For Men: Does She Hold the Divine Spark?

What should you as a man be looking for in this third asymmetry around mission? Girls did not pique my teenage son Thaddaeus's interest enough to date until he met Daphne. His experience with teenage women left him feeling that their minds were taken up with dumb things. But this woman turned his head because, besides being pretty, she had perspectives on things like family and church. In other words, he met a woman who had substance.

The question you might ask about your date is: *Does she have substance? Can she empower us with God's spark? Does she even have God's spark?* You can start with the query: *Does she have a prayer or devotional life?* I cannot advise falling in love with a woman who is simply needy. Our current social disintegration has birthed a crowd of cut and wounded women. The United States has the highest rate of youth self-inflicted injury. A 2017 study of tens of thousands of Emergency Room visits found that, from 2009 to 2015, the rate of intentional,

serious self-harm among 10-to-14-year-old girls increased
by almost 20 percent *per year*. Among 15-to-19-year-
old girls, the rate has been 7 percent *per year*.[65] Over the
period of 2001 to 2015 the rates for the younger girls grew
by 166 percent. And this is just counting the cases that
showed up in the Emergency Room, which means the
actual rate of self-cutting is much higher. These debutantes
of despair now coming of age are going to need a great
deal of patience and care from us. But I would caution
you against making that mercy a marriage project. If you
simply go for a maiden who needs saving, your life could
be limited in mission. Believe me, plenty of heroism will
be required of you in a relationship with even a healthy,
godly woman. Marriage itself is hard. Your patience will
be plenty tried. At this stage, have an eye out for a girl
who can contribute to the cause of Christ, the meaning of
life that you are trying to find.

* * *

Bruno, whom we met in chapter 1, had a history before
meeting swearing-off-guitar-players Joy. He once got
seriously involved with Jade, an attractive woman who
had a great winsome and creative spirit. They shared so
much together. The way he would describe it, he felt like
they just fit together, even their bodies in some mystical
way. One problem, though. Bruno became a Christian.
He thought for sure that Jade, who really was devoted
to him, would come along. She would be able to see the
value of Christ, especially as she was Jewish. After all,
Bruno thought, Jesus was the Jewish Messiah, wasn't He?
Jade even let him baptize her one night in a brook in the

dark. You can probably guess the sad ending to this story.
It wasn't pretty. Jade eventually had to be honest with
Bruno that she loved him but she didn't believe in Christ.
She couldn't build a life together around Christ. Bruno
eventually realized that he had to stop torturing her. They
broke up.

Some guys might press back here and raise the question, Why be so close-minded and prejudiced against a
mixed-faith marriage? If you really have found someone
that fits so well, someone with whom you just share so
much, minus your faith in Christ, can't it work sometimes
to build a marriage on that mutuality? Couldn't God
Himself be giving you this woman to perhaps influence
over time? Doesn't that sometimes happen in marriages
where one partner becomes a believer first? Couldn't it then
sometimes be fitting to begin a marriage with that hope? As
cited above to women, the Bible's answer here is no.[a] [66]

The reason, besides the practical and very real difficulty
of decisions about how to raise your children, lies in God's
desire for your love. He wishes you to be able to share the
deepest part of your heart with your wife. As time goes on,
the most important feature of your union becomes having
the same center of worship, that thing to which you both
give yourselves. Being disconnected there far outstrips the
commonality of watching the same sports or reading the
same books or loving the same games, or even holding the
same philosophy of life. I have pastored such "mixed-faith"
couples who eventually wake up to find that they cannot
share their centers. It becomes for the believing spouse an

---

a. 1Co 7:39.

unbearable sorrow. Let me tell you, you do not want to go there. In one church I pastored, a Christian man along with his nonbelieving wife played a prominent part in the life of the congregation. She was reasonable and cooperative, understanding her husband's passion for Christ. But she simply did not believe it herself. Every time a mixed-faith couple started to form in the church, I just sent them to have a conversation with this tragic pair to talk about their hearts' hardship. That usually did the trick. The singles were convinced to start with someone already going in a spiritually harmonious direction.

Gifted to Give Power

We saw in chapter 5 how prominently Psalm 110:1 plays in the Bible because of its description of trinitarian actions in our salvation. In the first Chapter of the New Testament book Hebrews, the author leads up to his[67] quotation of that verse[a] by citing the excellences of the second Member of the Trinity. One of those is how this One, the radiance of God's glory "upholds the universe by the word of his power."[b] The power the Beloved brings to the work of God upholds the very universe. It makes everything run.

This power is, for us, the feminine. When God first conceives of Eve, he calls her "Helper,"[c] a title that later gets applied to God in an expression of His power.[68] That means that the woman is like the Beloved, the Christ. She

---

a. Heb 1:13.
b. Heb. 1:3.
c. Gen 2:18.

is the divine empower-er of the operation, mirroring the divine Interrelationship. She powers the mission God gives to the couple. This becomes the model for us in coming together as couples. Thus, it is the wise boyfriend who spends time assessing his girlfriend's gifts and calculating how powerful they can be for God. As you date, it is appropriate to ask yourself if they would help in the areas of service you feel strongly about. It may not seem important now, but in the long run it makes an enormous difference in a marriage. You want a woman who can bring power to the mission.

How do you explore this? Try dates where you are doing some work together. I know many happy couples who actually first met in the midst of some ministry. It is neat when it happens that way. You are pursuing a call in some work for Christ and you look up and notice, hey, there is someone working next to you at the same thing. Olivia and Teja, from different churches, met at a prayer meeting. They are now enjoying a child they prayed to have. MaryAnn happened upon Ferris on staff helping to oversee a Young Life Camp. Ferris now serves as an elder helping to oversee his church with MaryAnn's support. Grayson and Savannah came together in an outreach to a despised people group in a foreign culture. They are now married, with two children, and thinking about how their family can address the plight of outcasts.

This is by no means everyone's story. But even if you didn't meet that way, you can make great dates of serving together. Ministries are always looking for volunteers. You might make a night of it. Patty (from the previous chapter), after leaving Boris on the hillside, came to appreciate her husband-to-be, Steve, while volunteering to care for folks with AIDs. They both showed up feeling a burden to help, as it was a great area of need at the time. Steve brought some medical knowledge with him. The ministry inevitably precipitated lots of conversation between them about life and death issues. They got to know each other in a distinctive, heart-revealing way. During one episode, Patty saw Steve fighting the administration for a dying woman's medication. This so impressed her, it just about sealed the deal of their ending up together. And they did. They just celebrated their thirtieth anniversary.

Around where I live, an Amish ministry sets up to process chicken for canning to go around the world in relief efforts. Volunteers can come donate time to cutting up chicken parts for the canning. It actually makes a great date. You recognize someone in an inimitable way when both your hands are bloodied with chicken parts. At the very least, such a date will inspire good conversation about each of your aspirations for service.

My son, Jeremy, carefully planned the January day he asked his wife to marry him. He wanted the asking to express what their marriage would be about, should his girlfriend, Hannah, say yes. So, he arranged a complete itinerary for the day. Much of it centered around food and coffee, an important part of their dating. He prepared a place for them to go swing dancing, which they loved to do together. But the day also included buying blankets and food, which they then distributed to some homeless people in their community. Even in his proposal, Jeremy

was conveying to his potential fiancé how he intended
their marriage to feature tangible service to Christ, an ideal
to which Hannah, fortunately, responded enthusiastically.
When he finally brought out the ring, she had a good idea
of what life with him would be like. And yeah, she said yes.

Growing Gratitude that 'No Living Man Is She'

One of the great delights of intergendered relationships
is learning how useful women are. You are probably
starting off farther along than I did in realizing this, but
the wonder of a deep love with a woman is coming to see
that certain battles only she can fight. Be prepared to be
surprised at how that divine spark answers needs in ways
that astound you.

The great moment for Merry, the hobbit, in *The Lord
of the Rings*, is when he hears the voice of the mysterious knight, "Dernhelm," ring out over the fighting, "No
living man am I." One of the deadly phantom Nazguls
had squared off against this lone, helmeted soldier on the
field. The cause of men is lost in the final battle of Middle
Earth, because the Nazgul is irresistible. No wizard can
destroy him. No elf or dwarf can fell him. No soldier can
face him because of an ancient prophecy that no man can
kill a Nazgul. Yet this one soldier still stands before the
beast over the body of the dying king of Rohan, ready to
fight. It is a fool's errand. Until it is revealed in the lines
above that opened this chapter that the soldier who stands
before the horrid creature is a woman. The prophecy said

nothing about women. Eowyn, with the hobbit's help, kills the Nazgul.

As Eowyn showed, certain victories are only achieved through a woman. I began to understand this when, early in our marriage, Mary K. and I had to get up early on an October Sunday and drive to a friend's wedding. I want to make it clear that I am not the kind of person who loses things or locks my keys in the car, but that morning it happened. I had brought some things down from our Brooklyn apartment to load the car, and, just as I closed the door, I realized that I had left the only keys to it inside. It was a very secure car. I returned to the apartment angrily contemplating how much I was going to have to pay a locksmith, if I could even find one at this hour, to come open the car for us, and how late this was going to make us. We were scheduled to play a part in the wedding; we couldn't spare a moment. As I, muttering, pulled a phone book off the shelf, Mary K. asked what was wrong. When I told her, she shrugged like it was no problem; she could get us off in no time. I asked how she could possibly do this. She explained that when she locks her keys in the car (which apparently happened all the time), all she has to do is get a wire hanger, bend it, and then go down and stick it in the side of the window and stand there wiggling it around, like she is trying to open the door. Within ten minutes, she explained, a random guy driving by will stop, get out, and open the door for her with some kind of tool. It would be a different guy each time.

I stood there for a few seconds staring at her in disbelief. Then I brusquely informed her that we could not fool around with such ridiculous tactics when we had a wedding to get to. We couldn't rely on some hope-for-the-best kind of attitude. We had to get it done the right way. So, I went back to getting it done the right way with the phone book, calling locksmiths that weren't open. Meanwhile, Mary K. took a hanger, bent it, and quietly went downstairs. I am telling you the honest truth when I say that it wasn't ten minutes. It wasn't seven minutes. It wasn't even five minutes. In less than three minutes, early on a Sunday morning, in a quiet corner of Brooklyn, a car came by and stopped next to my wife fiddling with a hanger in our car window. A guy got out of the car and opened the door for her with some kind of tool.

On that fateful Sunday morning, as I stood there by the car, it began to dawn on me that there were vast stretches of the universe that I could not fathom and yet to which my wife had access. We got to the wedding. No charge. On time. Mary K. was Eowyn, standing before the Nazgul, saying, "No living man am I."

On another October day, the evening of October 12, 539 B.C., to be exact, a similar fateful transaction of feminine singularity went down. Whatever his foibles and failings, the last ruler of the Babylonian Empire knew how to choose a wife. King Belshazzar was the one on the throne when Cyrus's general and the Persian army invaded and conquered Babylon. On that fateful October day, the unwitting king threw a party, which the Bible and other sources describe.[69] God tried to warn him, but the king couldn't understand the warning.[a] He tried via all his

---

a. Dan 5:1–5.

advisors to do it "the right way," all to no avail.[a] The only one who could help, it turns out, was the queen. At last, she enters the banquet hall and speaks. Only the queen could solve the problem by calling on the long-forgotten interpreter Daniel.[b] She was the king's last hope for averting disaster, but he was too foolish to see it. I have often thought of Belshazzar's queen while about to tell my wife how to do it "the right way." The Babylonian event just goes to show that, if ignored, a woman's singular saving power is to no avail. But that won't be you. Find a woman of substance. Sometimes, she is the only one with the answer.

The Very Long View

Here is another way to put it. Can you see your date getting behind God's call to your family to serve in the inner city? Or in Eastern Turkey? Or in prisons? Perhaps she hears a different call or, for one reason or another, cannot share the mission you see. Let her go. I am trying to help you take the very long view here. As Yoda once said, "Cloudy, the future is." The harder you peer ahead without really knowing what life will be like, the mistier it gets. But in that mist, your woman will be your power or your drain, your weakness or your strength.

The Old Testament book of Esther makes a big deal about the influential power of a woman in a man's life and his sphere. The whole story revolves around women's powerful influence with their guys' culture. First, the

---

a. Dan 5:6–9.
b. Dan 5:10–12.

Persian administration, the greatest power in the world
at that time, acts to remove Queen Vashti, after she disre-
spects her husband, because of her potential influence on
the culture of the empire.[a] This sets up one of the major
themes of the story: the strategic influence of the feminine. At a key moment that would make the difference for
their family and city, Zeresh pushes her husband, Haman,
down a destructive path of murder.[b] She could have
moved to change his direction, which would have saved
his life and the life of his sons.[c] Instead she encourages
Haman's prideful vengeance in a ridiculous plan to build
a seventy-five-foot gallows. As she eggs him on to punish
his opponent, Mordecai,[d] she sets the height of the gallows
to encourage, rather than contradict, his pride.

On the other hand, Esther delicately navigates the
court culture to save the people of God from genocide.
Her actions shift the sensibilities of an entire empire.[e] No
wonder the consequent holiday, Purim,[f] is still celebrated
by Jews today, over two thousand four hundred years
later.

God is not mentioned in the book of Esther, which
caused difficulties for some in accepting it as a biblical
book.[70] But others have recognized God hidden in it
behind the providence of events. The author may have
signaled this intent in the first Chapter, which contains a
phrase of four Hebrew words whose first letters, *HWHY*

---

a. Est 1:1–15.
b. Est 5:10–6:13.
c. Est 9:25.
d. Est 5:14.
e. Est 5:1–9:23.
f. Est 9:26–32.

form a reverse acrostic of the tetragrammaton, *YHWH*, the name of God. What is that phrase? In English, it is: "All Women Shall Give…"[a] Whether or not this code is intentional, the book does teach that God is made visible in women's giving. All women give through their influence, for good or for ill.[b] A few decades after Esther's victory, when Jerusalem lay in ruins, what we might call this "queen effect" seems to be the reason King Artaxerxes sends Nehemiah to rebuild the holy city.[c] We see the queenly power of influence, over and over.

This will happen in your marriage. Your woman will not be an accessory or a sideshow. She will be a power in your life and your scope of influence. Thus now, before marriage, you want to seek a woman that will be speaking with the right voice in your moment of vulnerability. You want a woman with her eyes on the prize of the things of God. You want, not a Zeresh, but an Esther.

So, woman and man, look here for these things growing in your date. The "growing" part means that he or she might not be quite there yet. Esther did not start out so well. In fact, she was pretty worldly.[71] She begins by acting against the Hebrew covenantal view of marriage, enthusiastically using her looks to get ahead[d] and concealing her unpopular Jewish identity.[e] She plays along with the courtly process and makes the most of it for herself. She struggles with doing right in the face of threats that-

---

a. Est 1:20.
b. "For ill," e.g.: 1Ki 21:1–25, 2Ki 9:7, 2Ch 24:7.
c. Neh 2:6.
d. Est 2:9; Est 2:13; Est 2:15–17.
e. Est 2:10.

jeopardize her position.[a] But, with time, a God-directed orientation arises out of her to match her shrewdness.[b] We are all works in progress. Your date is also.

If yours is the one for you, God has a purpose in bringing the two of you together. In many, many years to come, the quality of your married life will hinge on this question of mission. Each couple is different in furthering the kingdom of God in the world. Each has a different way of contributing to that cause. The adventure is finding out what that is, and then throwing yourselves into it.

---

a. Est 4:8–11; Est 4:13–14.
b. Est 4:16.

Meet the Family!

*When they sat down to supper, therefore, she considered it
a most unlucky perverseness which placed them within one
of each other; and deeply was she vexed to find that her
mother was talking to that one person (Lady Lucas) freely,
openly... In vain did Elizabeth endeavor to check the
rapidity of her mother's words, for to her inexpressible vexation, she could perceive that the chief of it was overheard
by Mr. Darcy... Nothing that she could say, however, had
any influence... Elizabeth blushed and blushed again with
shame and vexation... The expression of his face changed
gradually from indignant contempt to a composed and
steady gravity... When supper was over, singing was talked
of, and she had the mortification of seeing Mary (her sister),
after very little entreaty, preparing to oblige the company...
Mary's powers were by no means fitted for such a display;
her voice was weak, and her manner affected. Elizabeth
was in agonies... It appeared, that... her family had an
agreement to expose themselves as much as they could
during the evening.*
—Jane Austen[72]

Ruby: *Yeah, but... I thought you said your parents were in
Hawaii.*

Ron: *First Europe, then Hawaii.*

Ruby: *You know, Ron... we've been dating for three
weeks now... and all you ever do is take me to motels...
You wanna see me again? You introduce me to your parents.*

Ron: *Must you continually bring up my parents? — are you
getting out of the car?*

Ruby: *Yeah, I gotta go.*

—Spike Lee[73]

A Universal Rule

I tend to give a lot of background while giving advice. This may not suit your style. You may just want to hear the "how-to" instruction for dating. If so, I applaud you that you have made it thus far in this book. If you are the type who just wants the answers, I have here some more definite instruction.

"What should I do?" you ask. "Just give me an action to go to out there and perform every time." Well, if you want a rule, I have one for you. It is the one thing everybody dating should always do every time. As far as dating well, this is the most universal rule you could hold to, the most valuable act to understand your relationship and your future role in it. Unfortunately, this is also the most universally overlooked advice given on dating. What is it?

Meet the family.

After decades of social breakdown in America, increasing mobility of young people, and de-emphasis of parents in the process of dating, meeting the family of the person you are dating seems like an afterthought. Maybe it comes around after you are engaged and are planning the wedding. Perhaps you are not at that extreme, but you feel certain it only becomes important after things are serious, right? No, you need to switch the order. As soon as possible after you decide to pursue a relationship, *meet the family.*

Why is this so important? Once again, the answer is found in who we are. Because we are made in the image of God and because God is Trinity, so His very nature is

Persons-In-Relationship, it is in relationships that we, His image, are known.

The Same in Substance

Take Jesus, how wonderful He is. Think of just a few of the names the Bible writers came up with for Him: "Wonderful Counselor," "Radiance of God's Glory," "The True Light that gives light to everyone."[a] Maybe you have added some of your own. Have you ever wondered, *How come He is so dreamy like that? What made Jesus so great?* You really don't know until you *meet the Family.* Jesus is eager for us to do just that so that we could see Their pre-existent triune love.[b] His great qualities display what They together are. When we know the Father through Christ and experience the Holy Spirit because of what Christ has done, we see that all three of these Persons of God are of the same substance, *homoousios* as we saw in chapter 4. The experience of Christ's salvation is nothing less than being introduced to the triune personhood of God.[c] It is like getting invited over to your boyfriend's home for dinner, the ground floor of the family home.[74] From there we come to know the fuller glory of the divine household.[d] Granted, we might not ever see the upstairs or get a tour of the bedrooms, but we begin to understand what makes the Persons treat each other the way They do. The Family has a long history of enjoying one another,

a. Isa 9:6; Heb 1:3; Joh 1:9.
b. Joh 17:24.
c. Joh 14:21–23; Joh 17:3; Rev 3:20–21.
d. Eph 3:14–15.

long before you met Him.ᵃ And we see why that treatment is now spilling over onto you and how Christ treats
you. You get all this when you meet the Family.

In your date's family you will find out why this man
is so terrific and also why he is sometimes puzzling. You
will see whence this woman's strengths spring and also
why she at times grows distant. As you watch a man inter-
act with his blood ties, even if they are bloody, you can
learn volumes about his worth and his wounds. As you
observe a woman as she is in her parents' home, or with
her siblings, your eyes will see her personality anew. Just
the interactions stemming from your beau's birth order
yields volumes of insight. Because your date and your
date's family are of the same substance.

A Family Affair

Simply put, when you spend time with the family, you
can more deeply know the person. In the case of Cliff and
Kaylee, meeting the family actually made the match. It all
started when Cliff's brother married Kaylee's sister, Lydia,
and Cliff and Kaylee were naturally both in the wedding
party. The groomsman was utterly taken with the brides-
maid, but Kaylee, focused on getting her occupational
therapy degree, was not thinking about dating. And Cliff
himself did not feel worthy to ask her out. He didn't think
that there was anything inside of himself to love.

They saw each other at family gatherings, but nothing
seemed to happen for eight years. Yet things were indeed

---

a. Joh 17:26.

happening. Cliff was growing in Christ, becoming one who could "guard the gold," described in chapter 2. It took eight years for him to believe that there might be gold in him to guard, but Kaylee was still out of his league. It took the family's help to give him the courage to ask. Cliff finally admitted his feelings to Lydia, Kaylee's sister, and she encouraged him to ask Kaylee out. Lydia reasoned that both Cliff and Kaylee often complained about other people's attitudes toward singles, so, who knows, maybe they could do that complaining together. She was right.

When Cliff had "the talk" with Kaylee's dad, who was already something of an in-law to Cliff, they each knew exactly with whom they were dealing. Cliff understood the quality of his date's background, and Kaylee's father knew the character of this already familiar man. Kaylee still recalls the look of excitement on both her parents' faces when she told him that she had gone for coffee with Cliff. Her mother had had some reservations about a guy Kaylee dated in college and was lukewarm about that earlier relationship. Not so with Cliff. Dad and Mom were thrilled. Consequently, Cliff and Kaylee went from first date to conversations about engagement in two weeks. They have been married for several years now, in what you can imagine is a very well-connected family, and Cliff helps run a guy's group that addresses family issues for men. Your experience with your sweetheart's family may not be so determinative as Cliff and Kaylee's, but it can be just as informative in getting to know your prospect.

It is in relationships that we are who we are. It is especially in long-term relationships that we show, or don't show, godliness. And the longest relationships we have before marriage are with those we grew up with. They define a lot about us. Not to go too far afield, but this is why other significant decisions in the New Testament are tied to meeting the family. The apostle Paul warns that you should not dare make some man a church elder, one of the most important decisions any church makes, without first *meeting the family.*[a] The apostle also tells church leadership to make decisions on benevolent giving based on what is going on and what has gone on *in the family.*[b] When you are speaking about critical church decisions, the advice is clear. Your decision as to whether this one is the one is just as critical.

A Glimpse of the Future

Meet the family, not just to gain insight into your date, but to see your future, if there is to be one. Sabrina was so excited when she and William pulled into his father's driveway. She knew that William's dad was a prominent art professor at a major university and anticipated an illuminating evening. Well, she was right about it being informative, but not as she expected. Seeing the divorced father's lifestyle, and how he related to his son, she suddenly understood why William had a drinking problem. At one point, she was standing alone in a hall viewing the father's sex-saturated art. Certain things William had said

a. 1Ti 3:4–5.
b. 1Ti 3:10; 1Ti 5:3–4; 1Ti 5:8–10; 1Ti 5:16.

now took on great import. It clicked for her what life
would be like with the son. They broke up soon afterward.

If you are on the side of doing the introducing, you
might be mortified, as Elizabeth was before Mr. Darcy in
our interlude's opening, to have your own family exposed
to your date. Maybe you are not exactly proud of certain...
shall we say, features, of your kinfolk. But family and
future is not a simple calculus. A woman's background
does not set her future in stone. Just because her parents
got divorced does not mean she is destined by the stars
to the same fate. A guy is not bound by the dysfunctions
from which he arose. Just because his brother committed
suicide doesn't mean it has to run in the family. But if you
two want to understand the problems that your spouse
will be helping you with over the next twenty years,
should you marry, as well as the joys he or she will be
enjoying over that same time, you need to overcome your
embarrassment and let your date *meet the family.*

You can trace the lines of legacy into which you
are stepping when you meet the kin. How does your
date treat his mother? How does his mother treat him?
How do the parents treat each other? If there are unre-
solved problems, your date will carry them with her into
marriage.

Like Ruby in our opening quote, you may encounter stronger resistance in your date to an early exposure
to his family. You may hear, "You're dating me, not my
family! Leave them out of it." True. But again, because
we are in the trinitarian Image, we are who we are in our
relationships. You should plead the case by expressing this

as a desire to know him. She should understand this as really a quest to understand her. Spending some time with him in his growing-up setting doesn't necessarily mean that you will be spending a lot of time after marriage with them. You may form great friendships with them—which is fantastic when it happens—or you may not. Placing her in context is not a commitment to camp out there with her family forever and ever.

Your circumstances may also make familial connecting a conundrum. They might live far away. You might not be able to attend a Sunday dinner because there isn't a Sunday dinner. You might not be able to join them all together on holiday because his family is not all together. He might be estranged from his parents. There might hardly be any of her family left intact. None of these facts should deter you. As many and as much as you can, by hook or by crook, look for an opportunity to connect with them, and do it with your date present. Spend money if necessary. Take time off. *Meet the family.*

Finally, you might object that your own family members make too much of dates brought home too soon. Parents may embarrass you by acting like this is the one, or sisters might over-commit to a relationship with her before you feel that comfortable. But this problem is easily addressed by a conversation with the family beforehand. You can train them to understand that when you bring someone home, it is not a fiancé, it is just a date. They might never see the person again. Thereby, you can cultivate in them an appropriate, discrete friendliness. Because we are made in the image of the Trinitarian One, we are known through our long relationships. You will understand your date and your potential future more deeply than any other way by meeting the family. Are you looking for an idea for your next date? To answer the question, is this one the one for me, *meet the family.*

Part III
Am I the One?

It is good to see if your potential partner can perform the things from Part II for you. Can he or she fit you well? But marriage is a means of sanctification also. So, the testing going on is the testing of you too.

If you have read the previous questions for the opposite gender and nodded, saying to yourself, *Yes, I could do that for her,"* or *Oh yeah, I got that down for him easy,* you maybe can stop reading. If not, what follows might be the more important set of questions to ask as you date and think of marriage.

The questions are about whether you are ready. When Scott became a Christian at age twenty, he stopped fooling around and started thinking seriously about marriage. It seemed to be part of the package. Newly committed to a life of righteousness, he now wanted to do it God's way. His younger brother Sean was a big part of his conversion and, when Scott saw Sean marry and begin raising two beautiful daughters, he wanted to emulate that. Well, Scott dated for the next ten years with nothing ever working out. By age thirty-one, he had begun to think, *Maybe marriage is not God's plan for me.*

In a last-ditch effort on a Christian dating site, Scott met Sophia. This first date was different. He had a confidence at this point that propelled him. Because he liked her so much, he invited her to walk with him to one of his favorite spots, a waterfall in the woods. This was an unusual request for a first date—Sophia had just met Scott in person. But this date was different for her also. There was something very mature about this man. She decided to risk that he wasn't an axe murderer and took the walk.

It just clicked. Each came home from the date thinking: *I've met the person I am going to marry.* In this case, they were right! Though Scott proceeded prudently and they got engaged six months later, that unusual first night convinced them that this one was the one. What really crystallized at that moment? You might want to call it love at first sight, but, actually, it was a love for which God had been preparing each of them for a very long time. Things had not worked out for Scott largely because the ways he had learned to behave before converting to Christ continued as a pattern for him for a long time. Sophia herself had just come off of a very long relationship terminating in a painful but instructive end. She had changed through all of that. On that night, Scott was now ready for a wiser Sophia. Sophia was now ready for a great Scott. Are you ready for the kind of match God wants for you?

I am going to help you ask yourself the questions to find out. How do you do in making her secure? Do you think you could? Or do you seem to be able to bring him to a place of rest by your words, your deeds, or simply your presence? And can you be that firstborn for her? Can you step forward in responsibility for her sake? Or can you put him forward as a head, to surrender prerogative to him as a potential husband? And do you think you can find the purpose from God that encompasses you both? Or can you fit in that mission? Can you empower it? Can you practice these three asymmetries at all in your dating?

I bet you have been told many times that getting married will not solve all your problems. What you have been told is true. If you think that marriage will bring you only bliss, you are heading for trouble. It may not even solve all of your loneliness. But it is also true that God will use your marriage, if it is a good marriage, to bring you to glories you cannot even imagine now.

So, to get to a wedding day with the one who should be the one, let's go back once more, with a new focus, to the beginning.

Eight

Can I Secure Her? / Can I Give Him Rest?

Each man[75] will be like a shelter from the wind and a refuge from the storm.... The fearful heart will know and understand.
— *The Prophet Isaiah* [a]

Her ways are ways of pleasantness,
and all her paths are peace.
She is a tree of life to those who lay hold of her;
those who hold her fast are called blessed.
— *Solomon, son of David, king of Israel* [b]

For Men: Jesus Christ and King Kong

I was talking to my friend Seth after seeing Peter Jackson's movie *King Kong*, at the time (2005) the fourth highest-grossing film in Universal Pictures history. I expected Seth to like it, but he loved it. The reason was the scene where Kong fought not one, not two, but *three* Tyrannosaurus rexes. In the midst of having his arms chomped on *and* falling off a cliff, Kong battles these beasts—all while he is also keeping the woman, Ann, safe. Somehow he catches her, shields her from tooth and claw, and delivers her to a soft place, safe from each danger. In that scene,

---

a. Isa 32:2, (NIVO); Is 32:4 (NIV).
b. Pro 3:17-18.

Seth saw the man he wanted to be for his wife. I hadn't thought of King Kong that way (namely because it was a gorilla), but I appreciated the inspiration.

Christ's action for His bride, the Church, serves as an even greater inspiration. He cherished us[a] such that He went off a cliff, entering our fall with us.[b] Then He got chomped on to preserve us, in going to the cross for us. In terms of raw accomplishment, Seth saw in King Kong a visceral picture of what Christ did for us as our Savior.[c] Against unrelenting evil, He preserved His bride to place her on the solid ground beyond the cliff-fall. The apostle Paul says that husbands should seek to go as far for their wives.[d] You are not called to do that yet, with your date, but it is where you are heading, so you might as well practice to see if you can.

Making a woman secure. It sounds like a big job. But if you are made to do it, it can be surprisingly straightforward. Adam was made from the ground for Eve[e]—his name itself (אָדָם, *Adam*) is formed from the Hebrew word for *ground* (אֲדָמָה, adamah). He first grounded Eve with a name.[f] A simple act, right? But that name (אִשָּׁה, Ishah), derived from him (אִישׁ, Ish), secured her by giving her a context for her identity to unfold. In this way, Eve, though an individual herself, depends on Adam for help in knowing who she is. She came of Him. She can look to Him to know herself. You too can start to help a woman's

---

a. Eph 5:29.
b. Mar 10:45; 2Co 5:21.
c. Eph 5:23.
d. Eph 5:23; Eph 5:25; Eph 5:28.
e. Gen 2:7.
f. Gen 2:23.

identity unfold while dating. As you get to know her, you can describe to her what you see her to be. If it doesn't annoy her, you can even make up nicknames for her that call forth her value.

* * *

When Destiny and Darnell began dating in their twenties, they were both learning to navigate life on their own in the city. Destiny found herself in an awful apartment situation. Her landlord was mean and stingy and often threatened to sue her for repairs needed in the unit. When Darnell learned about this situation, he took it upon himself to call the scary landlord repeatedly and speak as Destiny's representative. The landlord then lit into Darnell personally, mocking him for thinking that he could help. Darnell did not actually accomplish much in the apartment situation with the phone calls, but it didn't matter. In Destiny's eyes, those phone calls accomplished the relationship. They have been married now for thirty years, and she looks at him with eyes that say it all.

Recall that this goes deep, because the Beloved is distinct from and yet comes from the Promiser. Again, these biblical names we are using for the second Person and first Person, respectively, help us see the archetype of gender in the Trinity. In the second New Testament presentation of the Gospel, the book of Mark, God does not figure as prominent a character as does Christ. But God shows up in the story in three crucial scenes,[76] in the beginning, middle, and end of the book. At the Beloved's baptism, beginning the ministry of life, the Promiser speaks to affirm His love.[a] At the Beloved's transfiguration, heading toward the ministry of death, the Promiser speaks similarly again, confirming the mission and endorsing the Beloved to the disciples.[b] Thirdly, the Promiser testifies, through a messenger, that the Beloved is raised from the dead. The risen One is vindicated.[c] These testimonies supported, interpreted and secured the Beloved at critical times of need. As we've said, God's action here gives us a glimmer of that which goes on eternally in Their relations, which gender imitates.

This is where your manhood is found. As things progress, can you do this for her? Perhaps she is not encouraging of heroics because she does not yet recognize how a man can secure her. That is okay. You can prove it to her with time. Perhaps you feel inadequate. That only means that you need to grow in skill at doing it. And you certainly can. If you find that you *are* doing it, you may be ready for marriage.

Not Even a Decision

The heroics of securing takes different forms. Amelia was a real prize. Able, beautiful, and spiritual, she excelled in her work and had already bought a house of her own. You could find her regularly in the nearby inner city, volunteering at a shelter—just one indication of how solid she was as a person. Jayden was duly impressed as he came to know her through their common circle of friends.

---

a. Mar 1:11.
b. Mar 9:7.
c. Mar 16:6.

But at the dinner party where they actually talked, she telegraphed that she wasn't interested in dating him (that is, she friend-zoned him). She didn't give him encouragement because, even though she had heard good things about him, he had dated her friend and they had broken up. That fact didn't give her peace. If you were Jayden, what would you do? Did a woman like Amelia need to be dazzled with a truckload of flowers? Should he impress her with a feat of physical strength? Should he volunteer more at church to demonstrate that he was spiritually minded? Take up nunchucks?

What Jayden in fact did was step back and wait for two years while he continued to encounter her in group activities. Eventually, he saw his chance when she moved into a new house she had bought and broadcast a call for help. After he helped her move into her new place, and then came over to set up her stereo for her, she reciprocated by making him dinner. Having him around her felt reassuring so she agreed to a date, and then another, and then another. After many months, they did pre-engagement counseling and were engaged soon after and married. The funny thing is, if she looks back, Amelia cannot recall a time when she decided, *I want to marry this man.* It was just that, little by little, in this and that, over time, she felt more and more secure by Jayden's presence. It was hardly even a decision. His actions made life feel firm. So he got her.

In fact, in a way, taking up nunchucks was what Jayden did. Nunchaku (nunchucks), the two sticks joined by a chain used in martial arts, was originally a Southeastern Asian agricultural tool. When the Japanese warlords forbade all conventional weapons, the Okinawans learned to use nunchaku as a weapon instead. While threshing their rice and soybeans, they were learning to secure their villages. Forbidden from direct romantic assault, Jayden did that also, using simple, steady, domestic acts as his securing weapon. Ten years and three children later, that security is evident in how Amelia talks about him. Can you do something similar? Does your gal call for this way of securing?

Girls Just Want to Have Fun

You can get started securing right away by planning a certain kind of date. "Girls Just Want to Have Fun" was a song that made a big splash for Cyndi Lauper a few decades back. In the song, Cyndi answers her parents who warn her against spending her nights partying and not getting on with her life. It goes without saying that the song (and official video) easily overcomes such stodgy advice with an exuberant dance number. By the end of it, we are expected to throw up our hands and join 1980s Cyndi in the street, then in her house, or even in her bedroom, casting off outdated notions of women wanting lasting relationship and accept that real girls, deep down, *just* want to "walk in the sun," with exciting hair instead of emotional attachment, to cavort in colorful clothing, with nicely matched accessories of course.

One might recoil from this characterization of women as superficial, but an important truth lurks within the lyric. On their second date, Trudy and Saul had the following exchange:

Trudy: So, why do you want to get married?
Saul (without missing a beat): For my sanctification.
Trudy (after a pause): Maybe you need to go read
Song of Solomon or something.

I'm all for serious conversation on dates, but this may
not have been the best first answer from Saul. Granted,
this was a mature couple, no longer in their twenties. His
answer spoke seriousness in his Christian walk and a
certain amount of maturity as to what marriage does for
us. Good. But this was the second date!

An important priority in dating is to make the date
fun and to look for opportunities to lighten up. Cyndi
Lauper may not have been right on an overall life plan.
But she has a point about dating. Dating is for having fun.
As the serious Christian dater that you are, you might
object. After all, we are seeking biblical priorities, right?
What could fun have to do with it? A serious Christian
should just be getting down to gender business on a date.
Not so fast. You will be doing serious business by making
a date fun. Why? Because in marriage (to which you are
heading, remember?) you will often find yourself as a man
called upon to convincingly convey one important simple
message. The message is: "Things will be all right." This is
hard when you are under pressure. Doing this in spite of
the pressure means a lot. It means that you are a real man.

Learn it now. All manner of real and perceived per-
turbations will daily threaten your family's peace. They
may require many different actions on your part. But
one thing they will always require of you. Again and
again. Over and over. Year in and year out. From day one

to day ten thousand and one. It is conveying: *It is okay.*
Not because of you, but because of the God in whom
you believe. His promises are unshakable, and you are
the bearer of that news. Whatever befalls your family,
and really whatever your wife's personality, they will be
looking to you for calm. They will be watching your tone,
your aura, your very eyebrows. And your job will be to
make it known: *Things. Will. Be. All. Right.*

You need training in your spirit for this. Better start
early: on dates. This is where fun comes in. The only
time people have fun is when things are going to be okay.
Hence, a fun date is a strong way of testifying that things
are okay. You are saying to her, "Relax! You don't need
to worry about anything." You are creating the calm. It
is you practicing being steady. Because it may take a lot
of practice. Inescapably, she will begin to feel secure with
you. She will feel like, possibly, maybe—just maybe—
there really may be nothing to worry about. You might
not even be sure what fun is. That makes it an adventure
for you—finding out what is fun for the both of you. It
will take effort and research to plan. But you can do it.

One of my most enduring memories is when I
brought Mary K. to get outdoor tango lessons at the
South Street Seaport in New York City. This was after
we were married a while, but things were difficult for us
at the church I was pastoring, and I wanted to reassure
her. So, I was still looking for a fun date for us. Now,
Mary K. is a real dancer. I am not, but I can enjoy moving
around a little on the floor with her while she does the
actual dancing. I will never forget the look on her face as

we tangoed outside on the pier. She was distracted in her usual way of fretting about many things. But I was leading so she didn't have to think about much. Then she looked up at the stars with this expression of marvel that I will treasure to my dying day. Her face was completely peaceful. Her whole frame exuded a sense of bliss. It was as if she was in Never Never Land. For those few moments, I really had convinced her that things were all right. As I say, I can never forget that look, and every time I think of it, I feel a great sense of bliss myself. This is the kind of moment you can create with a fun date.

There may be plenty of real things to worry about. There may be many real threats to things being okay with her. We are about to talk about one. But you must be the one to show the faith that says, "Even so, it will be all right in Christ." Because of what Christ has done, there is rescue. There is redemption. There is resurrection. You say that with your tone. You say that with your demeanor. And you can say that powerfully with a fun date.

It's a Hard Rain's A-Gonna Fall

Securing nowadays requires being extra heroic, King Kong-sized heroism. You should enter the current arena of women knowing that you may have a hard job ahead. The breakdown of gender and Western culture's turn from Christianity has brought about dramatic destruction in women. With men abdicating leadership for the sake of their women, women are left to fend for themselves, and without a society of caring men, they don't do so well. Significantly, studies say that women are less happy than they were even a few decades ago.[77] And one national study points to an elevated rate of rape or attempted rape on women.[78] The statistics of the prevalence of rape are hard to be certain about, but we can be sure that a society without faith is less safe for them. You may find your date to have sexual assault in her past. My wife has led several groups for young women through the years. When the discussion got very honest, when such things would come out, she was surprised by the frequency. So, the reality of women being hurt may be higher than you think. The recent "Me Too" movement has shone a glaring light on a sad situation. Such an event in your girlfriend's background can create a difficult-to-overcome deficit in confidence in you as a man. Can you respond to her particular needs and insecurities to ground her? Can you be the apple tree beneath which the Song of Solomon bride found shade?[a]

As you find out what makes her frightened, and then ask, *Can I address that fear?* you should realize that there are two basic ways. One is by shielding her from that fear. The other is by pointing her to Christ. Some worries run deeper than a concealed-carry permit can reach. Because they are found in a heart insecurity rather than a real-world insecurity. The best you can do for a woman in those cases is, as Paul instructs, to "wash her in the water of the word."[b] Her heart needs reassurance that can only come through Jesus Christ and what He has done for us. You are not a failure if what you say is not immediately received. Over time, women can get better, but they take patience.

---

a. Sos 2:3.
b. Eph 5:26.

* * *

Lauralee worked at a brewery together with a Christian guy named Gabriel. The restaurant offered employees a free beer after their shifts, and she and Gabriel got to sharing their post-shift beers together, talking about God. Gabriel would let her rage for a while and then patiently answer her questions. Through these discussions and this man, who was unlike anyone she had ever met, she reconsidered the claims of Christ.

The problem was Lauralee's past. The closer she got to God, the more she struggled with her own unworthiness and shame. When she and Gabriel started talking about dating, she didn't see how he could possibly come to love her. You see, Lauralee was raised in not just a secular family but an absolutely anti-Christian family. (When she started dating Gabriel, her mother told her she would rather have Lauralee bring home anybody, *anybody*, than a Christian.) She once walked out of a college literature class on the book of Job so livid with God's behavior in the book that she actually prayed to Him, even though she didn't believe in Him. She swore that only some act of ridiculous love would ever bring her to consider this horrid God of the Bible. Because of her family's worldview, her high school and early adult years were lived without restraint, a stretch of lascivious living and blackout drinking that she now summarizes as "just dark and ugly."

How could Lauralee be loved after her raucous past? Wasn't she damaged goods for someone like Gabriel, who would come to the marriage a virgin? It is generally hard on guys to find out that the one they are coming together with has been with someone else, or many someone elses, and Gabriel was no exception. But what Lauralee desperately needed, and what she found to her astonishment in Gabriel, was forgiveness. She says that his accepting her with her past was the greatest act of pardon anyone had ever shown her. It not only bound her to Gabriel, it convinced her that the gospel was true, that God was real, that love was real, and her family upbringing was completely wrong. It suddenly occurred to her one day that God had heard her prayer after the Job class. And He had answered it in Gabriel.

They have been married for nine years now. Lauralee still feels effects of her "dark and ugly" past, sometimes even in her dreams at night, and struggles with regret, but redemption has worked a growing radiance in her. Her husband's acceptance was how God did it.

Waiting for the Toaster to Pop

More serious matters of your own life may mean that you yourself have a ways to go to secure a woman. Vance had a daughter, Avery, about whom he cared very much. Avery took a liking to Colin, an honorable fellow who very much wanted to marry Avery. Both of them were under twenty years old, and Colin decided that the honorable thing to do was to ask Vance for permission to marry. Cool move, right? Usually, these kinds of requests go well because the father is so impressed with the guy for asking that the dad assesses this as a good match for his daughter. But to everyone's surprise, Vance said no. Vance talked with Colin, looked at some areas of his life, and honestly felt that Colin was lacking spiritually, such that marriage would bring some significant obstacles for them.

What follows such a devastating answer is often disastrous. In this case, though, Avery's relationship with her dad was such that she trusted his judgment. So in response, the two did not go off and elope. Colin, for his part, after he got over being furious, humbly took what Vance said to heart. The young man approached a pastor about it and began addressing what Vance had raised. It turned into a time, as Colin would put it, of spiritual awakening for him. Two years later, he and Avery, unplanned, happened to run into each other. They got to spending time together again. It wasn't long before Colin was back at Vance's door to ask again. Vance saw some real changes in Colin's spiritual life. This time, the father joyfully gave his blessing and the two joyfully came together. They have been in marital bliss for nine years now.

Not being there now does not mean that you are not going to be there later. You may be heading there and the toaster hasn't popped yet. Usually, a steady job is pretty important to give her assurance about you. Even more important is a certain amount of self-discipline. That is why the pastoral letter, Titus, when it gets gendered, mentions self-control and steadfastness a number of times for the guys.[a]

Down the line, you will find that securing a wife means attending spiritually to her children. Nothing brings more peace to a mother than this. If you have a

---

a. Tiu 2:2; Tiu 2:6; Tiu 2:7; and once for the women: Tiu 2:5.

demanding career, have you thought about how you will give time to children? Can you plan for it now?

But now, there is handling her spiritual state. You may need to ask, *Is her insecurity too deep for me to address by shielding (from harm) or pointing (to Christ)?* The answer could be yes. Allow that. If it is, you should consider ending it and fleeing like a gazelle. It could be because of you or her. Which one it is doesn't really matter in the decision to not pursue the relationship. But asking is very important in showing you how you or she may need to grow. If there is no woman that you can secure, you may need to take some steps as a man. If there is no man to secure her, she may need to take some steps as a woman.

As a parent, I felt like my kids dating in high school was fraught with the possibility of mishap. It is hard to do it right at that age and in that environment. So I set about trying to turn my three sons off to the idea of dating in high school. Do you know how I did it? I just kept talking to them about what a woman needs in a relationship. The more I talked about it, the more they felt overwhelmed by the whole affair. I got the idea from Jesus. He drew a similar reaction when He talked to His disciples about marriage. They replied: if it's so much trouble, it is better not to marry![a] In my guys' case, it was: if getting involved with a girl is so much work, why even date? For the most part, the strategy worked.

Remember, as we look at Jesus Christ, we find the paragon of masculinity in how He has handled the Church, His bride. No one has done more than Jesus to

---

a. Mat 19:10.

safeguard His woman-to-be. When we had no hero to
rescue us, tied to a pirate ship's mast of sin, He was a real
man for his bride. He swung across to the rebel vessel
and fought a troop to reach the mast. With one definitive
action, a strike against wood, our bonds were slashed.
Though He suffered—yes, really suffered—wounds in the
fight, He managed to battle His way to starboard side and
swing back, with us in his arms—that is, in union with
us—to heavenly safety. In ways we just couldn't, He did.
Because He did with us, you can with her.

~ ~ ~

For Women: The Delight of Footrest Making

As a woman in a potential marriage relationship, you
should ask, *Can I bring him down to that sleep that Adam
experienced, from which Eve was made? Can I bring him
to that "at last," "returning bone of my bone" moment?*
We saw in chapter two how Achsah ended up in the fairy-
tale-quality marriage with Othniel, the empire-killer.[a] But
the story doesn't end there. Achsah goes to work, making
a home for the two of them in a waterless place.[b] [79]

This kind of action began within God Themself. We
are used to thinking of the second Member, whom we
know as Christ, as masculine, because He took on a man's
body in human form.[c] And that is appropriate when we,
as His bride, think of our relationship to Christ. Remem-

a. Jos 15:15–17; Jdg 1:11–13.
b. Jos 15:18–19; Jdg 1:14–15.
c. Phi 2:7.

ber, from the perspective of some places, the relationship between the First and Second members of the Trinity can be seen also in the relationship between husband and wife. In this other metaphor, revealing other truth about God, we can see the actions of the Beloved toward the Promiser in a feminine light. It is not really how God is, just as, when we look at them in the analogy of Father and Son, we should not think that the human parental relationship is what they really are to one another. But our healthy human relationships carry within them the image of the dynamic between Them. So, in what has been revealed to us, do we see the Beloved acting as a Homebuilder to the Almighty?[80]

The prophet Isaiah put it just this way (as referenced earlier, in chapter 5). He had just finished describing the Messianic Kingdom, to which all of the earth is heading.[a] This won't be a place of weeping or calamity, but one where life is actually prolonged. Everything will be like God wants it. In this renovated world, even the wolf and the lamb will graze together.[b] This raises the question, Who will make the earth like this for God? Isaiah answers in the next verse:

> Thus says the LORD: "Heaven is my throne, and the earth is my footstool; what is the house that you would build for me, and what is the place of my rest? All these things my hand has made, and so all these things came to be, declares the LORD. But this is the one to whom I will look: he who is humble and contrite in spirit and trembles at my word."[c]

a. Isa 65:17–25.
b. Isa 65:25.
c. Isa 66:1–2.

The earth is to be God's "place of rest," His footstool. The only way this place of rest will come about on the earth will be through the Christ, humble and contrite in spirit. The Beloved will remake the earth to be, once more, a footrest for El Elyon, a place to rest His feet.

Let that imagery sink into your relationship. Your call to make rest comes out of God. With the right man, you have the power to renovate his world, to turn his deserts into a garden, to prolong life for him and fill him with delight. The Bible starts to sound Snow White-ish, with all this business of wolves and lambs cavorting together. But that really is what it is like when a woman enters a man's house. His wolves and lambs do start getting along. His air lightens. He sees in color. Those changes you bring are a little taste of what Christ is doing on a massive scale with God's whole earth. In this way, you are just like Christ.

It can begin in dating with the simple question: *What is the footrest for my guy? Am I able to make one for him?* My wife began simply with her lap. Early in our dating relationship in New York City, with little money, there were only a select number of places to go. We found a favorite spot in the north part of Manhattan at a park called the Cloisters. It had a castle wall upon which we would sit and talk. Because of my work then, I was often tired and started to nod. She would invite me to lay my head in her lap. This was a sacrifice on her part, because inevitably I would end up asleep, which killed the conversation. But she decided to lend her lap for this first act of rest-giving. For the next thirty years, she didn't stop. She just discovered other ways to do it.

Because this call comes out of God, there comes great delight in it. Recall that in the action of creation, Woman Wisdom is "rejoicing before him always."[a] The Proverbs passage sounds as if Wisdom is dancing before the Almighty as they create together, lost in the experience of being His delight. You will also find in rest-giving great rejoicing yourself.

Women's Work

A 2013 study published by the Pew Research Center found that, predictably, more than three-quarters of married moms would rather not work at a full-time job outside the home, preferring part-time work or full-time home-building.[81] Why would that be so? Because when you have children, your perspective tends to change. You develop a focus on the hearth. This draw certainly does not prohibit work outside the home, as the Proverbs 31 businesses and charities[b] and Paul's word choice in Titus 2[c] acknowledge. However, being clear-eyed means shrewdly observing how certain jobs better lend themselves to interruption than others. Just as men, as directed above, should eschew job choices that would make them bad fathers, you need to think now about how hearth-building fits in to a career. If you have career prospects as a woman, getting ready during dating usually means planning that career to be scaled back or suspended for children. With no such prospects, a man's salary or job security may rise higher on your dating

---

a. Pro 8:30–31.
b. Pro 31:14; Pro 31:16; Pro 31:18; Pro 31:20; Pro 31:24; Pro 31:31.
c. Tiu 2:5.

preference list. A couple's various economic needs, personal capabilities and individual circumstances make it hard to generalize about work-home situations. The cultural differences between the city and the country also limit the applicability of specific advice. So let me just recount some actual wise decisions to help you think ahead about your own future. The following women I know achieved that magical balance between work and home and active civic or church participation that grew out of their home.

Some I saw planned their vocational work to scale back when needed. Amy taught writing at a few different colleges. When she began a family, she was instrumental in helping her husband begin a new career. She then went back to writing at home, doing home-based writing work, and ended up working part-time as a lactation consultant. Margie was an urban general practitioner doctor with a husband who also had a decent job. She had a special niche visiting elderly shut-ins. Margie brought things to a place where, when she had her two children, she was able to set her schedule to only three days a week. She was able with this arrangement to hire a woman to help with the young children, someone they could trust to work closely with the family's priorities. The decision about using a nanny must be made carefully because the danger is always there that we are delegating out responsibilities that God has given to us. The presence of a hearth makes a difference in a child's life. But Margie wanted to, and did, very much remain the children's mother.

Rachel was a nurse who adopted, with her husband, Tony, several at-risk children. Tony was a church planter, which made his salary unstable. They did a wonderful job taking these kids in and raising them. Rachel found that by working just one day a month, she was able to retain her certification while devoting herself to her home until the children grew up. Not so for the doctor who delivered my second son. After doing a great job helping to give us our new infant, she told us sadly that she wished she could end her practice to be with her own eight-month-old, but she could not because of the liability insurance tail—she had to continue paying the insurance premiums for another fifteen years after she stopped practicing medicine, so she couldn't quit.

Other women are able to change their work to accommodate a family. Georgette, a lawyer, originally went into divorce law to try to break some glass ceilings for women. Sure enough, she found herself as a woman lawyer among a lot of men and encountered sexism when she got there. Georgette also felt the track to be difficult to manage with her growing family. So she transitioned to real estate law and was able to practice in a more limited way while attending to her growing daughters. Sharon was a solo musician actively pursuing a career in music. When she got together with Brad, that activity started to recede. Brad's work was slow in growing to a place of provision, and she found work as a worship music director of a church, which allowed her to have her children while giving them all stability. Later on, Brad's teaching position was able to take over in giving that stability.

Finally, some women just made the decision to quit. Natasha loved her work overseeing a counseling facility, and she was good at it. But her children took precedence and her husband, Alex, had the income to allow her to leave. She says that she is even happier now homeschooling their two children. Similarly, Margaret was a corporate attorney working that profession's traditionally insane hours. Her husband, Mason, landed a financial job that paid pretty well. So Margaret quit to have her baby girl. Margaret's parents told her that she was a failure for doing so, but, honestly, she didn't care.

I have seen many women, in areas requiring less income to live, flow in and out of part-time work, often centered on their children's schools, to support the family. They do quite well, happily working in gift shops, sewing, even raising chickens, which allows them a home focus. Some do critical work in the family business. Kay keeps the books for her husband's fence company. Ann does work restoring her husband's store property, while managing the home for charitable operations.

Whatever your situation, there is a way for you to grow into rest-giving, but it is good to think ahead. If you are living in America, you might pause and thank God for the flexibility that the country's economic system allows for varying income production. I have also found that when a man or woman makes a decision for the home, God providentially supports them in it.

Am I a Home Builder?

The main question right now is whether you can esteem this call. The Trinity's partnership in creation is brought

up in the New Testament as John begins his Gospel.[a] The
Speaker speaks. Then the Beloved Word, like a mighty
Executrix, makes streams flow and mountains rise. An
irresistible Force birthing worlds of splendor, the Word
expresses the Promiser's map. It is a glorious work.[b] This
is woman.

You may have obstacles to this creational work in
front of you. If, for example, you are prone to emotional
swings, you should spend the time now learning how to
recognize when you may not see the world as it is. Men
have their own hormone-inspired distortions (as cited in
the next chapter), but if you face this challenge, self-aware-
ness is important lest you tear down at night what you are
building during sunlight hours.[c]

Alternatively, you may not feel ready for all the
Proverbs 31 and Titus 2 stuff. Have you ever read that
Old Testament passage and, as you read, sunk farther and
farther down in your chair, wondering how you could
ever measure up? If so, that is all right. A lot can come
later. But get started on your dates making rest. The
responsibility stuff is merely an outgrowth of a homebuilder attitude anyway. The Proverbs 31 wife is a woman
who has been at it for a long time, and her home-building enterprises have just grown and multiplied. But it all
started long before in a simple objective to make a footrest
for a particular guy, and then his children.[d] As we saw, the
Titus 2 passage is about a home-focus, not a home-bound-

a. Joh 1:1–3; Joh 1:10.
b. Joh 1:4–5; Joh 1:14.
c. Pro 14:1.
d. Pro 31:12; Pro 31:15; Pro 31:21–22; Pro 31:27–28.

edness. You and your husband may negotiate the activities
of keeping the home. But if you do not have even the
objective to make a uniting hearth, then you are not ready
to date well. *How on earth do I do this?* you may ask. It
depends on the guy, of course. Are you ready for the
adventure of finding out?

Things Only You Can Do

Delight as a woman comes from grasping your unique-
ness. There are some ways only you can "homebuild." As
explained in Matthew 1:18–25 and Luke 1:26–38, God
became flesh through Mary's womb, but not proceeding
from sexual intimacy with a man. Our culture considers this
claim a humorous curiosity. In the theater where I saw Star
Wars Episode I (*The Phantom Menace*, 1999), when Shmi
Skywalker explains how her son, Anakin, was conceived
without any man—a backstory with obvious Christian
overtones—the line was greeted by peels of uproarious
laughter in the audience. But God is never arbitrary. This
singular feature of the real-life incarnation of Jesus Christ
proceeds from a profound necessity of our condition.

Ask yourself this: *Why a woman and not a man?*
Why not have Christ come through a man with the
wonder of it being that it was done without a woman? I
mean, so long as God is doing a miracle, he could certainly have done it that way. Why not leave the woman
out instead of the man? In fact, that might be even more
of a showstopper, don't you think? It might even top the
release of another Star Wars movie. And after all, men are
supposed to be so important in the Bible, right?

God wanted a feminine part to the story. But there was more to it than evening out the narrative or increasing the box office receipts. Mary's virgin birth happened because it was important to *not* have a man involved. You see, Christ came because we needed salvation. The first Adam (not Eve according to Romans 5:14 and 1 Corinthians 15:22, 45), was the representative head of us all. Adam was created first, so he was the head, the representative of the human family. It was his sin that doomed us, and we all sinned in him. This is termed *original sin*. Both our first parents did sin, but if Eve only had sinned and not Adam, would we all have been born with original sin? The correct answer is no. And if Adam alone had sinned and not Eve, would we all have been born with original sin? The answer is yes. Because Adam was the head.

The covenant of grace that accomplished our salvation, beginning in the birth of Christ, was a covenant between God and the man Jesus, as the Second Adam. Because the fully human Jesus was the second Adam (not the second Eve), He could act as our Head without sin. Unlike Shmi's kid in Star Wars, who turned out to be a real disappointment, Mary's child really was "The Chosen One." This new unsired one lived the perfect life as our new representative. So we receive His reward.

Thus, gender is very important in this operation. Man was the representative of original sin, so he could not beget the re-starter in the covenant of grace. The new man had to come without that original sin carrying man participating in the operation. This is not to say that His mother Mary was sinless—and here I know I part ways with my

Roman Catholic brethren—but that, as a woman, she did not carry the burden of the human family's representation. So, she could carry Christ in her body, making Him fully human yet born without original sin. We are saved through the femininity of Mary and the masculinity of Jesus Christ!

That is why God allows women, and only women, to bear children. Even with the very expensive operations that some men get to imitate women, they cannot, and will never be able to, become pregnant and bring a child into the world.

On this track you will find the other spiritual things that only you can do. It turns out that the major themes of the two-volume book of Samuel are introduced each time by women. Whether it be through Hannah's song at the beginning,[a] or Abigail's speech to David,[b] or the feminine medium's message to Saul,[c] or even Bathsheba's righteous appeal for her son at the end,[d] the weightiest matters of kingship come by womanly mouths. You are that woman at times. In taking the initiative to find out what relieves his load, what makes a home for him, what refreshes his bones, your critical gifts will come to the fore.

Are you able to rejoice in some homebuilding things that only you can do, such as being a mother or, as the Samuel women, giving voice to life themes? You aren't doing that yet, but can that distinction inform your dating decisions?

---

a. 1Sa 2.
b. 1Sa 25.
c. 1Sa 28.
d. 2Sa 12:24; 1Ki 1.

Nine

Can I Take Charge for Her? / Can I Esteem Him?

*And they heard the sound of the L*ORD *God walking in the garden in the cool of the day, and the man and his wife hid themselves from the presence of the L*ORD *God among the trees of the garden. But the L*ORD *God called to the man and said to him, "Where are you?"*
— The Prophet Moses [a]

The woman said to him, "Sir, give me this water, so that I will not be thirsty or have to come here to draw water." Jesus said to her, "Go, call your husband, and come here."
—The Apostle John [b]

I hail this man, the watchdog of the fold and hall; the stay that keeps the ship alive; the post to grip groundward the towering roof.
—Clytaemestra, to Agamemnon[82]

For Men: No More Days Off

Jack and Kate were parked in the brown mini-station wagon in Fort Tyron Park, one of the beautiful bastions of green in Manhattan. They had recently gotten serious in their dating. They had also just been eating ice cream and were feeling really good. They started to make out. It was getting hot and heavy. Jack suddenly protested, "We've got to go." "Is there something you have to do?" Kate asked?

---

a. Gen 3:8–9.
b. John 4:15–16.

"No," answered Jack. "Our Father wants us to stop."

This question, *Can I be in authority?* is prone to be misunderstood because Christian authority in relationships is misunderstood. It is caricatured as being about who gets to hold the remote and decide what to watch. It is demonized as *The Handmaid's Tale.* Many ignore, or just don't understand, what it means to be in charge the way that God asks us to be in charge.

If we call it being a "head" in the relationship, as termed by the apostle,[a] then it is not about a will to power. It is about laying down your life for her sanctification. It is about caring when you don't feel like caring. It is about dealing with her problems when you are tired of them. Yes, being a head means that you have a certain privilege of setting the agenda in the relationship. But that also means that you cannot take a day off from said privilege.

What does this mean in dating? It means, first and foremost, taking the lead in not sleeping with her before your marriage. In the Bible's terminology it is refusing *porneia*—that is, sexual activity outside the life-long covenant.[b] At the very beginning, your true masculine leadership is here shown, or surrendered. To keep the time honorable is your essential act of headship in dating. This area as the place to start "heading" may not be immediately obvious to you. There may be lots of other things you want to head in. But this is the most important. How come?

As we have talked about, sex is great in its time, but not before the promise. The promise has not yet been

---

a. 1Co 11:1–16 or Eph 5:22–33.
b. First Corinthians 6:13; First Corinthians 6:18–20; First Corinthians 7:2; and Galatians 5:19–21 are some examples of the word's use.

made when you are dating. The promise has not yet been made when you are engaged. You've made a promise with that ring, maybe, but not *the* promise. Words are cheap. Sweet nothings whispered in the darkness are just that—nothings. Even the ring, even if it was anything but cheap, is cheap. The promise happens when you stand, with the church presiding as God's representative, before your families, your friends, the world, the flesh, and the devil, and pledge your life-long, sole commitment to this woman. It happens when you enter into that thing called a covenant with her—what marriage is[a]—and imitate the commitment of God. It happens when you mark the moment Jesus intended in saying, "God has joined together,"[b] when that joining is publicly and socially proclaimed. Then, and only then, is the promise made.

In a dating relationship that is going well, you are getting closer all the time. That is good and right. But then sex becomes difficult to avoid. Remaining what we call chaste is especially hard with the limited accountability of modern life. If you press her, she will likely yield. Eventually. Again, if things are good between you, she doesn't want to resist you. If you push for it, you'll probably get what you want. But in that win, you will have lost something of immense value. You will have made an indelible mark on her mind: she will now see you as one who is controlled by desire rather than conviction. She will know, firsthand, that you are likely to trade long-term profits for short-term gains, swapping away the kind of lasting value for which marriages strive and upon which marriages are

a. Mal 2:14.
b. Mat 19:6.

built. In her mind, it will become enormously difficult to shake the idea that when push comes to shove, and you want something that she may not, something that may not be good for her, the answer will lie only in what you want: your will over hers.

That impression will form her response to you in the arguments that you will have. In that one act, you have established a crippling pattern of relating that will be very challenging to overcome. You've gained a conquest, or some premature pleasure. But you've failed to be a man. You've lost trust. And without that trust you have just made marriage that much harder.

But if you take charge by conveying your intentions, making a decision with her about what is right and helping the both of you to stay true to it, you have won a deep respect. You have set up a marriage life in which she will look to you for guidance. And she will learn the strange urgency of your desires and want to see those desires fulfilled. So you will probably have sex quite frequently.

Just as importantly, you have shown her how costly she is. Knowing that she is worth waiting for will ground her like nothing else. It says to her: you deserve the promise from me. That knowledge of her worth, which you can give her with this masculine move of headship, will make a profound difference in your life ahead. A woman who knows her worth is a fountain of life to those who live with her (meaning, you). A woman who can really believe that she is precious, not just mouthing it from all the self-help trumpets selling her aromatherapeutic candles, but truly believe it from your act of waiting for her, this woman will be a treasure of feminine gold. You can give her that by this first, simple step of self-sacrifice.

So, the decision to remain chaste with one another and stick with it really rests with you. Sometimes we hear it said that it is the woman's job to say no to inappropriate physical touching. This idea is properly termed *hogwash*. It is the woman's job only if the man abdicates his. Now, if you have fallen already, all is not lost, as the story of Al and Elektra in the next section shows. At each juncture in your walk together, you can take steps into headship. But if you are wise, you will set up accountability now for both of you to stay true to a decision about physical engagement. Because it is not easy. The best serious relationships make themselves accountable to family or friends.

There is another reason to start talking about this matter of sex up front, before you have it. It will set up a good pattern that is essential to good marriage: talking about sex. This discussion among married couples is often lacking, which is amazing considering how important sex is. But good sex takes practice and a lot of communication. You will need to be speaking about what is possible, what makes each of you feel good, and what hurts. So, it is best to allow it as a general conversation topic, even before you start doing it.

The Rep Gets the Rap

The next step of headship is courageous representation. When Adam and Eve sinned in the garden, God seeks out the man to give an account. They both blew it, but it is

Adam's name that rings out among the trees as God walks
along in the cool of the day. He calls to the *man,* not the
woman, to explain what went wrong.[a] He wants Adam to
give an account, to represent them and their actions. The
buck stops with the husband. This is what you are stepping into.

It is also why the prophet Hosea, during the Assyrian
crisis of the eighth century B.C., prophesies against the
men but not the women in his message of judgment. His
heavily gendered book depends upon an analogy of marriage infidelity to convey how God's people are rejecting
him. As the memory of the Davidic covenant fades, they
all, men and women, are behaving pretty awfully. Yet the
prophet narrows in:

> I will not punish your daughters when they play the
> whore, nor your brides when they commit adultery;
> for the men themselves go aside with prostitutes and
> sacrifice with cult prostitutes, and a people without
> understanding shall come to ruin.[b]

The men will be punished. The women will not be. God,
through Hosea, holds the men responsible for this bad
state of affairs because the men in the covenant community are the representatives.

✴✴✴

One Sunday after church, Al approached me looking
very heavy. He said that he and his fiancé, Elektra, had
to speak to me in private. It had to be both of them, and

---

a. Gen 3:8–9.
b. Hos 4:14.

it was urgent. I was at a loss for what they could want to talk to me about, but he was clearly upset. They were one of many young couples who were getting together in my church. These were two sincere, committed Christians who really wanted to do things right. So, in the Gothic building we were renting, I found a small room—really more of a dusty, elegant closet—where the three of us could sit down alone. The cramped talk was obviously quite difficult for Al, but it eventually came out that they had slipped and slept together. He was asking me whether they should break the engagement off, or suspend it, or what. During the confession, I was listening to Al, but I was watching Elektra, especially her body language. She was very quiet, feeling ashamed of course, but also uncomfortable that they were doing this. When I saw this, I was relieved. Because what I really wanted to discern was this: Who's idea was it to take the uncommonly brave step of coming to confess to their pastor? While I was not happy that they had jumped the gun in their physical relationship, it wasn't a good reason to change their direction. Instead, I was eagerly looking for a sign that Al was leading in their repentance. From what I could tell, he was. He was taking responsibility in an area that most men would rather shirk. This indication of their trajectory reassured me. Al, though having sinned, was establishing a pattern of acting from conviction. I could express hope for them and encourage them forward from there, with hopefully greater accountability. This year they will celebrate their fifteenth wedding anniversary.

This same responsibility is called forth when a

woman at a well asks the Messiah for the water of life.[a]
Jesus doesn't refuse her but asks first for her husband to
come. He knows, or will discern, that she has no husband,
but He still asks the question as appropriate to the interaction.
Some might get annoyed with Jesus here for calling
for the husband to be involved. Cannot Jesus deal with her
as an individual? Jesus does speak with her first as an individual.
Then at a certain point, He feels that her marriage
(if she had one) comes into play. Masculine representation
is necessary for an intergendered relationship to work.
Can you, oh modern man, leave the life of a saddle tramp
for this kind of life? Only then are you ready to date and
marry.

A Man or a Muppet of a Man

If you want to see a real man, look at Christ in this relationship
to His bride, the Church. Jesus took charge for
us even when we were apathetic and unappreciative. He
wielded rightful authority when it was most needed, and
people noticed and were astonished.[b] He did the kind of
things that make us say, "Whew. I am glad he is in charge.
It is so needed!" And He knew exactly when to lay that
authority down too.[c] He represented us by dying in our
place.

You are not in that place yet, but there are some initial
ways of moving in this asymmetry while dating. Now is
the time to ask, *Have I matured enough as a man to have*

---

a. Joh 4:10–16.
b. Mat 7:28–29.
c. Mar 10:42–45.

my own opinions? Am I able to be decisive about things while taking her concerns into account? Can I represent another whole person, and especially this person? Some of these answers depend on her, of course, but we have already talked about that in chapter 5. The question is now about you. If you cannot be decisive, or cannot do so in a considerate way, you may not be ready to be a masculine dater.

Dates are wonderful places to see how you do as a head. Can I ask her out with a direct question, rather than "Hey, do you want to hang out together sometime?" Am I willing to be the one to step forward to buy the tickets? Now, who buys the tickets is nothing in and of itself. And you should not do it to cultivate passivity in her. But it can be used as a small step to see if you can take responsibility for two. What about a potential plan for dinner? You should always make sure that you have a design for her to eat, even if the gallivanting is spur of the moment. Maybe it is easier for her to check if the restaurant is open, or call in a reservation, but you should make sure that there is a plan.

Take the important step of gathering her thoughts and comparing them to your own. Does she have allergies? Does she have food preferences? It may take some work to extract what she herself honestly wants. Supposing it is different from your own preference, how are you going to handle it? What is the principle of righteousness you are operating on? Dating is a dance displaying your willingness to sacrifice desires for the sake of the marriage and future family. Buying dinner at the restaurant she likes can communicate this. It is a symbolic courtship ritual. It says, "What you desire is important to me." If she loves seafood and you hate seafood, can you first give up your preference for her benefit? On the other hand, can you devise a long-term surf 'n' turf arrangement to try to help you both appreciate each other's preferences?

Try to enjoy your call to take charge for her. If you find that she enjoys surprises, have fun planning a date without telling her much about it. I planned my first date with Mary K. to be a surprise visit to an ice-skating rink on top of a tall city building. I'm not a very good ice skater, but she turned out to be a pro, so, thankfully, it was great. Husbandry is growing things. You may later realize that, for your particular woman's growth, she needs to learn to plan an outing, to change the oil, to cook dinner or to manage a stock portfolio. Depending on your mission (discussed in chapter 10), you might even be called to offer stability and encouragement for her to run for Senate.

These are some ways you can begin to take charge for her benefit. Dating is a chance to see if you really can do it the way God wants you to. Can you step forward for her?

When Mamma Ain't Happy, Ain't Nobody Happy

Another of the most important ways is in the ability to contradict her. "When mamma ain't happy, ain't nobody happy." That is what my fellow elder said to me many years ago. I found the expression abhorrent. It describes how a wife or girlfriend, when her will or opinion is

defied, has ways of making a guy's life miserable until
she gets her way. I didn't disagree that the condition was
common. It draws a smile of recognition when spoken.
The saying actually appears in the Bible, in another form.
And it is repeated several times:

> It is better to live in a corner of the housetop than in a
> house shared with a quarrelsome wife.[a]

Yes, it is all too common in marriages. I did not object
to the saying. But I objected to how this elder, an older,
supposedly wise shepherd, was speaking this saying to
justify dropping a matter of rather bad behavior of a man
in a church. Don't stand against this action, he advised,
for the man's wife is for it. And she knew how to make
everyone's life miserable. But Proverbs' recognition of
the dynamic is not a call for a guy to therefore yield to his
woman's wrong opinion. Instead, such times are a call to a
guy to stand for what he sees as right regardless of domestic consequences. A lot of guys have trouble with this,
even if they believe their wives to be wrong. She might
scream or she might softly manipulate. Eventually he is
trained to follow the path of least resistance.

Instead, consider righteous Job. The narrator of
the book of Job goes to great lengths to establish just
how righteous Job is, both before and even after his
trials begin. After their misfortunes strike, Job's wife, an
important figure in the tragic story, says to him, "Curse
God and die."[b] It was tough. She had just lost her chil-

---

a. Pro 25:24. Consider also Proverbs 19:13; Proverbs 21:9; and Proverbs 21:19.
b. Job 2:9.

dren to catastrophe and, with equal suddenness, a great deal of wealth through the vaporization of their proper- ty.[a] But she did not respond well. She weighs in on how they should interpret the matter and respond. Her view? "Curse God and die." What often goes unnoticed is how Job rebukes her. "You speak as one of the foolish women would speak," he retorts.[b] Job refuses to interpret life according to her words. Basically, he is telling her to stop speaking. Interestingly, Job's wife, albeit a main character in the story, does not speak again in the book.

This, however, added trouble to the already suffering man. Later, Job talks to his friend, Bildad, about how he has become repulsive to his wife. She won't even toler- ate his breath.[c] In other words, she will not allow him to come close to her. Figure out the meaning there. Even so, even denied her bed, Job held to the decision to defy her and her counsel. He would not take her view, or allow their actions to proceed upon it, come what may.

If you are a man with a woman in your life, you must be able to ride out the storm of her wrath. This is what it means to bear authority. And when husbands cannot restrain the faithless words of their wives to others, the consequences are usually disastrous, and not just for their families, but for anybody standing nearby. There is a time when you must be able to refuse the fruit she offers.[d]

Yet when a husband learns to bear this test, the situation is transformed. Job explains to Bildad what is

---

a. Job 1:12–21.
b. Job 2:10.
c. Job 19:17.
d. Gen 3:6.

happening in Job's marriage in Chapter 19, right before a critical moment. As he stands in this decision, perhaps one of the hardest parts of his trial, the sufferer arrives at his crucial life understanding, then uttering the most important line in the book: "I know that my Redeemer lives."[a] Not coincidental.

Not only that, the woman herself will often be profoundly affected by a close man who can and will defy her for what he believes is right even though she disagrees. Things weren't over for Job and his wife. They have ten more children, seven sons and three daughters, in fact.[b] That fact not only tells us about Job's health. It also tells us about the health of his relationship with his wife. It tells us that he came to be received into her bed again. It tells us that their relationship deepened through his stand for insisting on God's way. At this stage of dating, you just need to ask yourself, *Am I a man? Can I defy her? What is the result?*

Everything's Legal in Jersey

On the other hand, your good defiance can bleed into bad "overbearance." As I mentioned earlier, Mary K. has, from the beginning, had a desire to respect me. But I did not always take that respect well. One day, I was leading a caravan of cars from Brooklyn, New York to Middletown, New Jersey. It was the pre-cell phone and pre-GPS time of history when people actually relied on writing down directions and reading maps and stuff. In this utterly primitive era, along with our cave fires and

---

a. Job 19:25.
b. Job 42:13.

spearhead carving, getting lost was a real and common cir-
cumstance. I had the stressful job of trying to keep these
cars from all getting lost. I was doing this by staying at
the head of the caravan. My fiancé was driving one of the
other cars. At one point on the highway, because she must
have felt that I was going too slowly, or as a joke, or for
whatever reason, she pulled ahead of me. I felt a great need
to keep the lead of the caravan, so I pulled alongside her
car. I started making faces at her. She just started laughing
with the others in the car, which led to me making more
exaggerated faces. After a few minutes, she realized that I
was angry and pulled back.

A friend in my car who watched all this took me aside
and compared what happened to some other interactions
he observed. He explained that he was troubled by how
I was treating my fiancé. I was making her submit, rather
than trusting God to let her submit. It was the beginning
of a needed repentance in me. I had a girl who wanted to
respect me. I didn't have to make her.

Are you prone to anger? Do certain circumstances
bring out a beast in you? Have you begun to recognize
that what flows through your veins in those times sometimes colors your eyesight so that you don't see straight?[a]
Have you learned to consider your words carefully in
those Hulk-like moments? Can you be overbearing when
you take authority? Do you assert your will in pride or in
caring responsibility? How about when things go wrong
on a date? Can you step forward when there has been
some failure, regardless of whose fault it was? Can you

---

a. Jam 1:20.

identify with the problem, even if it wasn't your doing? Can you demonstrate forgiveness when needed? If not, you may not be ready to be a husband.

~ ~ ~

For Women: God's Image Lite?

And you, dear woman reader, what is your question on this path? It is to ask of your heart, *Can I put him forward to this place of taking charge for us? Can I strike a posture of submitting to him? Can I so esteem him?* It may seem arbitrary to you. *Why should I be the one to submit? Is there something inferior about me?* The answer, of course, is no. There is nothing inferior about you. You are made in the image of God. Get this part straight first. Many women grow up with a sneaking suspicion at the back of their minds that they aren't really made in God's image. God is always presented to them as masculine, so... maybe they are really just God's image-lite or something.

Go back to the Book. The first Chapter, as we saw, says that being made in God's image made them male and female.[a] Meaning, *ipso facto*, God is epicene. The Lord contains within Themself the archetype of the feminine *and* the masculine. This is confirmed in the New Testament:

> Nevertheless, in the Lord woman is not independent of man nor man of woman; for as woman was made from man, so man is now born of woman. And all things are from God.[b]

---

a. Gen 1:27.
b. 1Co 11:11–12.

Note that last sentence. These things are, literally in the Greek, "ἐκ τοῦ θεοῦ" (*ek tou theou*) or "out of God." Man and woman, the masculine and the feminine, come out of God. Both find their origin in something about the Persons of God. Thus, you come out of God as much as men do. That is why, as feminist theologians are always quick to point out, God is at times represented in the Bible with the feminine. I count more than a dozen passages of varying lengths where this is explicit, including many individual verses.[83] So yes, God must include what we know as the feminine as well as the masculine.

But, you object, the overwhelming majority of biblical references to God are masculine. Why? Because gender is about relationship. In a book about our referring to and relating to God, God teaches us to address Him as masculine because of the asymmetry of order. We are made to promote Him in the biggest way, to put Him forward to His rightful place of ultimate authority. As C. S. Lewis put it, "What is above and beyond all things is so masculine that we are all feminine in relation to it."[84] Yes, in the sense that we are called to make the earth His footstool, a place to rest His feet, to enable His work in the world as defined in His covenants, and to yield to His will. So, Israel is pictured as the bride of YHWH[a] and all followers of Jesus are envisioned as the bride of Christ.[b] He is Husband, Lord, as well as Father, to us all.

So yes, you are God's image. You do not submit because you as a woman are inferior. Nor is there something about your nature that makes you better at

---

a. Isa 54:5; Hos 2:16–20; Hos 11:2.
b. Joh 3:28–30; Eph 5:31–32; Rev 21:9.

submitting than a man. God has submission in all of our
futures, but in different ways. Similarly, God excludes
men from different activities. As we discussed in chapter
8, men are shut out from the exalted and essential privilege of childbirth. It doesn't matter if a man really wants
to have a baby, or feels like he ought to have a baby, or
stamps his feet and shakes his fist at the moon, crying
bitter tears at how it is not fair that he will never have a
baby. It is not going to happen. You, on the other hand,
were not made the firstborn. You were made to be in relationship with that firstborn. It is the relationship nature
of gender that makes it hard to speak of promoting in the
abstract. You may need to have a man in front of you for
you to envision what that means.

Scribbled in Dark Ink

I'd like to show you something that belongs to my wife. I
carry it around because it helps me appreciate where she
has come from and the wonderful person that she is. It's
a reproduction of a page from a copy of a book that was
hers before she got married.

　For you to appreciate this, we need to note the
twentieth-century author, whom I just quoted above. The
book is called *Mere Christianity,* by C. S. Lewis. I'm
willing to bet that you've heard of the book, if not read it.
Certainly, you've heard the author's name. He is pretty
famous. In fact, he is famous in a certain way. Among
Christians, no one ever criticizes C. S. Lewis. You're not
allowed. He is quoted and re-quoted, but never maligned.
He occupies a certain position, probably because of the

exemplary life he lived and how helpful his books have been to so many people. But whatever the reasons, you will likely never hear a Christian put him down or even offer a mild correction, much less cross something out in one of his books. And certainly not in his most famous book of all. That is what makes this page from my wife's copy of *Mere Christianity* so striking.

In a very brief passage late in the book, Lewis gently suggests, with painstaking care I might add, that possibly, maybe, men and women might have different "roles" in marriage—that is, that they might love each other differently. Those last words are mine, not his, but that was the gist of it. At that point, this young unmarried woman's pen went to work, as you can see.

Note the force of Mary K.'s ink lines. You can tell how heavy the hand is on the pen. Originally, the motions that made the marks were so violent they almost tore the paper. Today, I cannot think of another woman who more thoughtfully embraces the Bible's teaching on wives with their husbands than my wife. She exemplifies holy promotion in a relationship, the kind she used to attack, as shown in that book page.

What accounts for the change? It was because she got close to a man. It is tough to embrace the Bible's teaching as a single woman because it is often hard for a woman to imagine the goodness of submitting to a man. Until she loves one. Then it starts to make some sense. A good relationship with her father makes it much easier. If, while growing up, she knows a man who cares for her and has seen the value of submitting to him, it becomes better. If she has brothers she has wanted to promote to responsibility, or felt good attention from brothers in Christ in her church, she is even better prepared.

But ofttimes it finally clicks when this man to whom she may tie her life, whom she really wants to succeed, whom she really wants to be a man, stands in front of her, and she can see the effect of esteeming him. If putting forward one you love still does not make sense to you, I need to ask you, for you need to ask yourself, *Is this an area where I need to grow? Am I ready to be married?* Because being married means taking on man, with all that man is.

Part of your problem may be misinformation. Perhaps you associate the Bible's teaching here with things with which it does not go. Nowadays it is common to believe that the Christian ideology of husbandly authority and wifely deferral creates a climate of male domination and female subservience, that it discourages men from being expressive with their wives or promotes domestic violence. The good news is that this is a fallacy. If you get with a Christian churchgoing man, statistically you are far less likely to find yourself in an abusive situation. This is not widely known because it does not fit the current cultural narrative, but it is nonetheless the case. Research indicates no association between conservative Christians (or even religion in general) and domestic violence. Rather, "churchgoing conservative Protestant men register the lowest rates of domestic violence of any group" in American households, based on three different national data sets.[85] So, find out with an actual God-honoring guy what is really involved in this practice and what is not.

Should Women Be Quiet?

Again, you do not love this way because you are less in worth. There are secondary sexual traits that make men and women in general better or worse at one thing or another but that is not what promoting is about. Instead, it is a matter of meekness.

The funny Greek adjective πραΰς (*praus*; pronounced something like *pra-oose*), which means "meek," appears four times, three of those times in the Gospel of Matthew.[86] The first occurrence of πραΰς is in the famous beatitude "Blessed are the meek, for they shall inherit the earth."[a] The other two times, Matthew is describing Jesus Christ.[b] The only other time this word in adjective form materializes is in the first letter of Peter, when Peter is talking about women. Why is this word used to describe the acts of Jesus and women? Well, it has to with the meaning of meekness.

It is a great Christian virtue, but it is also an important tool of femininity. Not in the twisted way it comes across in caricatures of Christian marriage. Meekness is not being silent while being abused in a marriage. You sometimes hear preachers intone, preaching a sermon on meekness, "Meekness is not weakness... even though the words sound

---

a. Mat 5:5.
b. Mat 11:27–29; Mat 21:5.

similar!" This is so. Meekness is the fantastic power to not do something you could do. Not from natural reticence nor from being oppressed nor from feelings of inferiority. It is the choice to not do for God's purposes. And this takes great strength. This is why real meekness is a characteristic of Christ and one of the most advanced of Christian virtues, a marker of greatness. It is very precious in God's sight, and He is going to give the earth to those with it.

What is the mark of a great basketball player? Not only being able to shoot but knowing when not to take the shot. Look at the choices of Magic Johnson or Steph Curry. Unbelievable shooters, yet they know the moment to pass to another team-member. Maybe they could make the basket, but they choose not to. So how does Peter actually say it about women?

> Do not let your adorning be external—the braiding of hair and the putting on of gold jewelry, or the clothing you wear—but let your adorning be the hidden person of the heart with the imperishable beauty of a gentle [meek] and quiet spirit, which in God's sight is very precious. For this is how the holy women who hoped in God used to adorn themselves, by submitting to their own husbands.[a]

Why does Peter, like his fellow apostle, Paul, at times,[b] tell women to be quiet? Is it because women are not as good at speaking? Or is there something about men in general that they should talk and women should not? Or

a. 1Pe 3:3-5.
b. 1Co 14:33-35; 1Ti 2:11-15.

are women not as able to discern good doctrine? No and no and no. Neurologically, women tend to develop more of the brain in the area of verbal fluency.[87] Statistically, women speak more words during the day than men. So, generally, they are pretty good with words.

No, it is rather because in some relationship contexts, God asks women, because of their hope in God, to refrain in order to promote their brothers or their husbands. That is why all Scriptures advising women to quiet behavior also make reference to a husband. God asks a woman to leave space for her man to fill. And in the filling, something important happens in the man. Something even more important happens between the two of them. Womanliness, like manliness, is about relationship.

So Peter, in using the word *meek,* is actually making a strong statement about women's equality. He is telling us that there are needs in the relationship that her refraining addresses. Not because of what she cannot do, but because of what she could but doesn't. That's meekness. In this context, that is womanliness.

Logan and Hazel are a great couple. Earlier in their marriage, Logan had to make a costly business decision. They talked it through but Hazel, his wife, was still against it. Logan decided to go through with it anyway. The business venture failed, and it set them back quite a ways. To this day, Logan practically comes to tears as he explains what happened after. Which was nothing. Not only has Hazel never once said, "I told you so." She has never even brought it up. The decision to accept it even if they failed was part of her submission in the first place. Her forbearance meant so much to Logan, it changed how he saw his wife. It changed him. I wasn't there when this all went down, but I have to tell you, when I look at them now, I see an uncommon partnership. That business loss formed them. They are also doing fine financially.

This may still seem tricky to live out in your situation. Maybe you know more about the Bible than he does. What then? You can be a Priscilla, a knowledgeable woman noted in the Bible, not as a teacher, but as one who helped promote a teacher. [a] Maybe you have more experience or knowledge in some areas of your lives. What then? You can be a trusted advisor. Maybe you are simply a better decision maker than he is. What then? You can still do it by helping him to become a better decision maker for the two of you. All this makes the man as he learns to trust the wisdom in the voice of his wife, something God often tells husbands to do. [b]

The real question for your heart in dating is: *Can I delight in his taking charge for my flourishing?* Because that is key to being a woman. If not, if you find you are more like Clytaemestra in *Agamemnon*, who speaks the nice words above but secretly resents Agamemnon, you need to explore why that is. And you need to do it now. Take your time. Understand yourself.

Can I Submit to Somebody?

Dates are a great place to find out how capable you are of respect. Sometimes we hear someone say, "I'm just the

---

a. Act 18:26.
b. E.g., Gen 21:9–12; Pro 8:1–15; Pro 31:26; Pro 31:28.

kind of person who speaks her mind." Well, okay. But this is no virtue without caring discretion. Being able to say what you think is not always courageous. Sometimes it is just self-indulgence.[a] Rather ask, *In what I say, is it easier for me to find fault or to encourage? Am I able to show respect to this guy? How good am I at conveying faith in another's ability to lead? In a close relationship, am I quicker to instruct or to appreciate?* That is where you will find your womanliness.

✵✵✵

Revelation Media's 2019 3-D animated version of *The Pilgrim's Progress* presents a funny but helpful picture of this. In this wonderfully done rendition, the wife of Giant Despair, named Diffidence, can't help but criticize her giant husband. Yet when she does, he faints and becomes inoperable. Pretty true-to-life, actually. Struggle as Diffidence does to encourage him to the work, she cannot hold her tongue, and blasts him for being such an oaf, which brings the giant to a faint. His collapse provides the way of escape for Christian and Hopeful. While we are happy to see this happen in the story, we are grieved to see how often this dynamic plays out in real-life relationships, limiting their forward movement.

If you see him try to make a decision for the both of you, can you praise him for it, even if with subtlety? Supposing it is not the decision you would have made? Does that really matter? If things go wrong, can you be gracious about it? Maybe those words "I told you so" are on the tip of your tongue. Can they stay there without passing

---

a. Pro 10:19.

through your lips?[a] Perform a little experiment while
dating. Note how many decisions in the relationship came
up this week. It is not important for him to make every
decision, but of all of them, how many did he handle?
Could he do it without being overly controlling and while
valuing your opinion? Of those, how many were ones for
which you expressed some appreciation?

These things might seem trivial right now. But that is
the point. What movie you see or which way you drive
to the Superbowl party usually are trivial. The stakes are
low. That is the beauty of dating. You are baking in a way
of relating. His sense of your esteem is anything but trivial.
Decisions are coming that will have high stakes. Very high
stakes. At those moments, your relationship must carry
you both. How you relate to one another will determine
how things go.

Let me clue you in. Most serious arguments between
married couples seem to be over trivial things. If you ever
try to help a couple to reconcile when there has not been
a serious betrayal, you will find yourself amazed at how
they could get so upset over so little. One time, I was
helping a couple who were fighting over how to mow
their lawn. One might be tempted to say, "Come on! Are
you children? Are you really unable to work this out?"
But the wise counselor sees that the issue is usually not
the issue. The issue of the argument, such as who should
have taken out the garbage, or whether you changed the
cat litter, is really about deep matters of respect and care.
Those matters are based on the patterns of relating you

---

a. Psa 141:3.

begin in dating, when the decisions do not really matter. This is the place to find out: *Can I be a promoter?*

Can I Bring My Whole Self to Engage with Him?

There do also come those moments when, as a matter of right and wrong, you say no to him. Biblical submitting means helping him discern righteousness because, ultimately, you both must submit to God. This requires your full engagement. If a boyfriend asks you to do wrong, can you say no as you should? It may be that he asks you to outright lie about a real estate property he is donating to charity.[a] Or it may be more cloudy, perhaps in the area of physical intimacy. You may need to oppose him in the back seat of the car. Can you do that well? In faith, not in fear? Early on, if you allow yourself to be pressured into sleeping together, you are destroying the foundation, setting a pattern of relating that will be very difficult to overcome. In issues that arise during dating, can you be respectful but not cave on matters of right and wrong?

When I speak publicly, I often like to play with the audience by giving them a quiz, for a book giveaway or something. One of my favorite questions for Bible readers concerns the time when God was making Old Testament Israel into a kingdom. The promise that God makes to the first great king, David, was not only that his throne would be established in Israel, but that a son of David would hold that office ever after. The royal covenant was

---

a. Act 5:1–10.

a covenant of dynasty, to provide righteous rule through all generations. Pretty important point in the history of our salvation, no? So, I like to ask if anyone knows the first person in the Bible who speaks that promise, not just that David will be king, but that he will have a dynasty? It usually takes an audience, even a biblically literate one, a long time to guess. Do you know? The answer is Abigail.[a]

If you are looking for inspiration in how to graciously contradict a man doing wrong, consider the great queen of this first great king, (and the one who should have been his only queen). Abigail shows her nature in 1 Samuel 25, before she becomes David's wife, while married to another man, who sins in refusing to help David, the Lord's rightful anointed one.[b] She manages to righteously contradict both her husband and her future king in the same Chapter. David sees her goodness and later, when she is widowed, sends to her for marriage.[c] Likewise, in interactions before marriage, you show your true colors by how you handle difficult situations like this one.

As I said, there are times of saying no to even a great guy. If you find yourself having to say no too many times, this may not be the guy for you. If you cannot find enough raw material in him to respect, maybe you should look elsewhere. Escape like a bird from a fowler.[d] As we spoke of in chapter 6, now is the time to decide if you are dealing with someone you will be able to esteem. Being not married is better than being married to a man unwor-

---

a. 1Sa 25:28. The Hebrew term *bayit ne-ehman* (בַּיִת נֶאֱמָן) that Abigail uses in this context means, as some translations make clear, a lasting dynasty.
b. 1Sa 25:2-35.
c. 1Sa 25:40-42.
d. Pro 6:5.

thy of any respect. But if the answer is always no, if there is no man on earth to respect, it may be that you are not ready to be a wife.

* * *

Lilly was a charming young woman in my church. Smart, beautiful, considerate. I had the utmost respect for her family and their faith. I enjoyed watching her take careful steps in a new dating relationship with Fred. I did not know the guy, but I hoped he understood the value of this girl. In discussion about it, she shared with me how Fred had a besetting problem. She courageously supported him, doing all she could to help him overcome this obstacle. I told her I thought that she was a great example of laying a sound foundation for a future marriage. But she also came to understand that, in the end, we cannot will someone to change. Despite all our help, we cannot enter or share in another person's heart.[a] Her beau persisted in his problem and would not change. Lilly's brother, Eli, who had been counseling her all along, eventually advised her to cut bait. They weren't seeing enough of a response in the guy. Fred was just not able to show change in this serious matter. But Lilly was earnestly looking for a man to respect. Today she is married to another worthy guy. Eli and I are delighted to say they are very happy. Maybe you are like Lilly.

We all, including my wife and I, tend to err on one side or another in trying to get this asymmetry right. Many husbands I know either don't know how to take charge or tend to take charge for their own good rather

---

a. Pro 14:10.

than their wives's. We err on the side of passivity or dictatorialness. Most wives either idolize their husbands or tear them down. How to do none of these as equal image-bearers takes a long time to learn well. But we can be way ahead of the game if we are asking how we are doing at it during dating.

~~~

For Both: How to Be Happy

Americans have a misconception that we can make ourselves happy. Maybe it is because we have enshrined the "pursuit of happiness" in our government documents. But you do not actually become happy by pursuing happiness. Man or woman, right now, you don't think the things that actually do make you happy will, and you think that some things will make you happy when they actually won't. Your desires may seem immutable, but they are not. If they are aberrant—that is, outside the covenant of marriage that God has for us—they are not your true self. The more you lean into them, the more they can feel like they are part of you, but they are not. Following God's way for us changes even what we thought was our identity.

I once found myself in a very painful conversation with Mark, an active member of the church I pastored, and a friend. He was in my office explaining to me about his background. His mother was abused in Catholic school, which turned her off completely to religion, so he was raised outside of any church. He told me that in sixth grade he marched into the kitchen and told his mom that he was gay. He knew it then. Mark went on to have several relationships with men in college. When a woman friend, Rosalita, shared the gospel with him, he told her that he could not be a Christian because he was gay. But she encouraged him to nonetheless press on in coming to Christ, which is how he ended up in my church. He was trying to make both work. Now, here Mark was, having been with his current partner, Brian, for a year and a half, telling me that he and Brian were sacred treasures to one another. They were prayer partners, Bible readers, and considered themselves a Christian couple. There was no other way for him but in this relationship. I told him respectfully that what he thought wasn't true. God always has a way for us to turn from what He tells us is wrong and to fulfill what He tells us is right. Mark disagreed. He proclaimed that he cannot change being gay, and he could no longer lie to God about it. He left the church to be with Brian.

Recently, I had breakfast with Mark. We both happened to be in New York City while he was doing a job there. Now many years later, I was glad that he was willing to reconnect. I discovered then that Mark was married to a woman, had three children with her, and couldn't stop talking about this family. He insisted on showing me pictures of his wife and kids. In fact, I found it a little annoying because he kept wanting to show me more. I mean, the children were cute, but he seemed to have an encyclopedia of photos on his phone, with each of them wearing funny hats from multiple angles. Enough already. I say that, yet I wasn't really annoyed. I was happy for him. This same man sat in my office years before, looked me dead in the eye, and insisted, "I was born this way and can never be different!" Well, apparently not.

Whatever desires you treasure, even those ones that seem to be a part of your identity, are not necessarily so. Even your patterns of physical arousal, if they are aberrant, can change, as the Bible[a] and honest sociologists acknowledge.[88] And even your vision for self-fulfillment, if contrary to what Christ tells us, can take a strangely new shape. Acknowledge this deficit in self-knowledge and you will make better dating decisions. You may not see how it works at the moment, but if you become a man, which means treating this woman you are dating as a woman, or if you become a woman, which means treating this man as a man, then you will, with time, whether with this other person or not, find yourself in great bliss.

True happiness in life comes about through strong relationships. The Harvard Medical School's Study of Adult Development is one the longest longitudinal studies on a single cohort ever performed. This comprehensive study, generating tens of thousands of pages of data from these lives over decades, showed that good relationships are what keep people happy. High-quality, close relationships, especially marriage, are what makes people happier, physically healthier, mentally sharper, and able to live longer.[89] Such close relationships are sustained by doing them God's way. So happiness, it turns out, is something that sneaks up on you as you treasure God.[b]

---

a. 1Co 6:11.
b. Mat 5:3–12.

Ten

Is There a Mission for Us Together? / Can I Empower Our Journey?

Thus says the LORD, "I remember the devotion of your youth, your love as a bride, how you followed me in the wilderness."
—The Prophet Jeremiah[a]

*Hellish anguish did [the knight's] soul assail
To drive him to despair, and quite to quail...
Una saw...and to him said, "Fie, fie, faint-hearted knight-
What meanest thou by this reproachful strife?
In this the battle, which thou vauntest to fight
With that fire-mouthed Dragon, horrible and bright?*

*Come, come away, frail, seely, fleshly wight,
Nor let vain words bewitch thy manly heart,
Nor devilish thoughts dismay thy constant sprite.
In heavenly mercies hast thou not a part?
Why shouldst thou then despair, that chosen art?*
—Edmund Spenser[90]

For Men: A Life of Getting On with God's Purposes for You

Finally, discerning dating means taking personal steps of purpose. King David, before he died, instructs his son, Solomon, on becoming a man. The great ruler tells his

---

a. Jer 2:1.

son that being a man is finding out what God has said and what it means for your life.[a] Solomon had a number of problems to solve to become a man, and relying on God's covenant promises was a big part of how he did it.

Sometimes we need the charge, such as David gives to Solomon, to get on with things. That needed prompt is no score against manhood, for it is actually doing the things that make the man. Caroline was a director of an important department at a shelter, and Leonard met her in the midst of his social advocacy work. He was honest with her about his unwanted same-sex attraction, but they were so aligned in mission that they just hit it off and began dating. Leonard came from a background of severe relational brokenness. His own father and mother were never married, and he had few examples to follow in this intergendered relating thing. So he was not skilled in moving forward in the relationship. After almost two years of dating Caroline, a guy in his small group challenged him to not leave her hanging. Leonard responded by making the dangerous decision. In a beautiful ceremony in a Brooklyn park, Leonard sealed the deal with Caroline, and they have been successfully exploring marital bliss ever since. It is taking the steps forward that make the man, regardless of the help he may need in taking them.

You also discern the mission by addressing problems. If you are addicted to pornography, you show leadership in tackling that problem before getting seriously involved with a woman. Porn will destroy any relationship, and if

---

a. 1Ki 2:1-4.

you have become enmeshed in it, you lead now by chart-
ing your way out. The longer you have been in it, the
longer it takes to wash yourself of it, but it can be done. It
takes bringing your problem to others in your church and
getting help for yourself. You are doing this for her, even if
you haven't met her yet.

One of the best ways you can prepare for marriage
is to get a sense of your direction in life. This will better
allow a woman you are dating to discern if and how she
fits. I was not the best example of this order. I was slow
to get a calling because certain matters between my father
and me had to be addressed first. Mary K. was instrumental in that healing. She generously encouraged exploration
through different jobs. Eventually, long after, I was prepared to enter vocational ministry. She helped me hear
the call. The wise woman of the Old Testament town of
Abel averted a war because she went "in her wisdom" to
Commander Joab and he listened to her.[a] In that case,
leadership meant recognizing and adopting the better idea.
But it would have been better for Mary K. if my work and
direction in life had been established first.[b]

As an Eagle in the Sky

After bringing mission-mindedness into your life, it is easy
to let it come out in your dating. The book of Proverbs
reaches its youth-training climax with the final Chapter's
advice on finding the best wife.[c] In the lead-up, we find

---

a. 2Sa 20:14–22.
b. Pro 24:27.
c. Pro 31.

one of the less-read verses of Proverbs, concerning the physical "way of a man with a virgin:"

> Three things are too wonderful for me; four I do not understand:
> the way of an eagle in the sky,
> the way of a serpent on a rock,
> the way of a ship on the high seas,
> and the way of a man with a virgin.[a]

To penetrate the meaning of these words, we should caress the points of comparison between the phenomena described and the last "way"—that is, sexual intercourse. The writer, Agur,[b] uses the first three physical rhythms to elevate the act of sex. The movement of all four is mysterious and marvelous, but especially so is marital intimacy. Each of those first three things names the pure medium against which a beautiful creature or creation finds its glory. When do you see an eagle being what an eagle should be? When it has taken to the sky. When do you see the glory of a serpent's body? As it ripples across the rock. When do you see what a ship was made for? When it is sailing the high seas. In fact, if you hoisted a ship out of water and put it on land, without the support of the water, it would just fall over. So likewise, when do you see a man being what he was built for as a man? In coming into a physical relationship with a woman.

Agur's words are a great counter to monogendered relationship by giving us one of the reasons that it is not

---

a. Pro 30:18–19.
b. Pro 30:1.

God's way for us. As he considers this bodily sign, it is too
wonderful for him to understand. As we have discussed,
sex is never just about sex. It is a sign of a deeper dynamic
between the man and the woman. The "way" of the man
is to act upon and move on the woman. This shows how
man was meant to be. As you act in the context of woman,
your nature comes forth. It doesn't really come forth with
another man, but with a woman. You were made to move
on her.

Start with an easier question. The first mission, the
first purpose, is asking her out. Do it straightforwardly.
Ambiguity is everywhere. You can show yourself a man
by dispelling the ambiguity and being clear that you want
to date her. God assists a guy who makes dating a mission
in sometimes striking ways.

***

Olivia was dealing with some trauma in her background,
and a recent dating dead-end, so she was not receptive
when Teja approached her in September after the prayer
meeting with "I like you." All she could say was that she
had had a relationship that did not work out and she was
not ready for one now. She did not feel it was fair to tell
Teja to wait because she really did not know when or if
she might feel ready again. Teja made the dating enterprise itself a mission. He pursued her from a respectable
distance for a few months, giving her time. He eventually
decided in prayer that if she did not relent by March 19,
he would consider it a sign that this was not God's initiative. He would terminate the effort and move on. But
he did not tell her this. As his private deadline drew near,

providentially, Olivia's work took her to the Indian Ocean, in the region where Teja was born. While there, in his ancestral homeland, something began to change inside of her. She returned and, three days before the cutoff point, she let him know that she would like to be his date. Now married and new parents, they spend their days wondering at the child coming from this "way of a man with a virgin."

Later, you grow into this "way." Once you are dating, can you discern God's purpose for this date? Maybe it is just to have fun, or maybe that and something else. Why not pray about it? As time goes on, start to ask that as a bigger question: *For this month? For this year? For our lives together?* Apprehend the mission.

Jesus-and-Us Was Never Just About Jesus and Us

I make an effort to meet with each couple that I marry one year after the wedding. I want to see how they are doing and check if they need any help. Usually, at that point, they don't. They feel like they have this marriage thing down, like they are now old pros. But I also want to ask them something — chiefly, the guy. My year-later question to the newlyweds often surprises them. I ask, "What is God's purpose for your marriage?" That is, I want to hear why they think that the Author of Love brought them together in love, why He gave them each other. Because we think of marriage as a big enough deal in itself, we usually do not take the further step to ask that question. But your marriage, if you do marry, will have a mission.

You must find a woman who, underneath it all, pri-
oritizes mission over her own happiness. Nora and Chris
looked like the couple that would always be together.
Chris's father, a minister, did their engagement counseling.
They both were regular churchgoers and seemed to carry
a strong Christian confession. Yet one thing remained
true about Nora: she was sure that God wanted her to be
happy. Her own parents had been divorced. Now there
is nothing that says that a woman with divorced parents
cannot have a successful marriage, but when they split up
Nora learned that the pursuit of happiness was the priority. Though she insisted, as many do starting out, that
divorce was not in her vocabulary, there were other things
in her heart that would later loom as a greater lesson.
They had the struggles that most young marriages have,
as two people try to forge a life together. A child laid a
heavy burden on the young parents, as a young life is very
demanding. An attractive man "friend" came along at just
the right time of difficulty, with a repeated refrain that
resonated with her: "God wants you to be happy." Sure
enough, Nora at last decided that she could be happier
with someone besides Chris. And because God wanted
her to be happy, she divorced her husband and split the
family. The sadness remains for Chris and his daughter to
this day.

God has a greater purpose for your marriage than
just you being happy. Each couple is different. Each has
a different way of contributing to that mission. But the
mission part is not optional. Though this question about
the point of your marriage is a simple one, that doesn't
mean that it is an easy one. It may take years to figure

out. My goal with my one-year question is to encourage the husband to think about it, look for it, plan in a way to find it. Why? Because any marriage that is just about itself eventually goes sour. Just like any life that is just about itself goes sour as well. God made us each for a purpose of service to His kingdom. And He made our marriages just so likewise. Thus, I coax newlyweds, after a year of self-focus, to start connecting their love to the purposes of Christ. You can set up for that connecting, however, by how you date.

Why would mission be a part of marriage and dating? When we look at God, we find that the union of the trinitarian Persons, perhaps like the first year of marriage, is completely self-contained and self-satisfied in Themself. They had no need for a greater purpose beyond Their own blissful fellowship. The Trinity in eternity is like a newlywed couple. They don't need anything beyond each Other. They could get snowed in for two months and hardly notice. And yet, we find that this love was pleased to find expression in outward acts. The first project we know about was creation—when They made everything. Another we call redemption—when They saved everything. In that second one, our salvation came out of a series of promises They made to each other, something theologians have called the *pactum salutis*. And the point of it is that God made Their union into a good purpose that went beyond Themselves.

As Christ's bride, the church's masculine Head leads us in a mission, keeps the sights steady, and is willing to correct us when we get off the track. (I do not know how many wives lose focus about the marriage's mission but, honestly, the church does quite a bit). He shows us the will of God for the work of the church. He gets it done by fostering our gifts to make the most impact. It may not seem like that is what He is doing all the time, but that is because we are not taking enough steps back to see it. Christ makes some mighty strange moves with His people, but it all serves His aim of making disciples.

When we come to our romantic relationships, then, we find the same principle to be critical for a healthy relationship, beginning with the formation of that relationship in dating. You and your wife both coming to the table with well-defined careers can be a great boon to your life together. But along with this blessing may come a greater difficulty in answering this question of your union's purpose. I do not know what God's purpose for your future marriage will be. But I do know one thing: God is not giving you the gift of marriage so that you can each pursue your separate jobs and touch base once in a while to have sex and check on the kids. No, your marriage has a mission. As a man, you have a special call to find out what this mission is. Just as the first man got the call,[a] so He has a call on you, Adam's son, as well. Thus, mission-mindedness must enter into your dating. If this one is the one, God has a purpose in bringing you together.

What is an example of a marriage mission? For me, and then me and my wife, and then our whole family, the prominent theme was cultural engagement, using what we had to build bridges between our current American

a. Gen 2:15.

culture and the church. This vision enfolded many factors, including my gifts, my wife's gifts, and our context living for many years in Washington D.C. and New York City. The theme helped me to say no to some opportunities, yes to others, and helped us decide how to spend our time. With my young children, for example, it gave the impetus for the family producing a *Star Wars: Phantom Menace* study guide, to discern the truth in the popular culture offerings of the time. The project took a lot of effort and drew puzzled expressions from many in our church at the time. But it fit with our mission. If you are a believer, Christ has something important for you to do. You will need help. Go find it.

~ ~ ~

For Women: Can I Empower the Mission?

Acts 18, the one place Priscilla of Rome enters the New Testament narrative, suggests an interesting pattern for Christian women toward close men in their lives:

> After this Paul left Athens and went to Corinth. And he found a Jew named Aquila, a native of Pontus, recently come from Italy with his wife Priscilla, because Claudius had commanded all the Jews to leave Rome.... Now a Jew named Apollos, a native of Alexandria, came to Ephesus. He was an eloquent man, competent in the Scriptures. He had been instructed in the way of the Lord. And being fervent in spirit, he spoke and taught accurately the things

concerning Jesus, though he knew only the baptism of John. He began to speak boldly in the synagogue, but when Priscilla and Aquila heard him, they took him aside and explained to him the way of God more accurately. And when he wished to cross to Achaia, the brothers encouraged him and wrote to the disciples to welcome him. When he arrived, he greatly helped those who through grace had believed, for he powerfully refuted the Jews in public, showing by the Scriptures that the Christ was Jesus.[a]

When Luke introduces Priscilla,[b] he cites Aquila, her husband, first, respectfully giving him the masculine representative role in the family. In fact, Luke and Paul always mention Priscilla along with her husband.[c] Especially if she does have a prominent teaching place in this story, this conjoining to Aquila affirms the asymmetry of authority from Genesis, that the husband represents the couple. However, she is named first the other two times in Acts 18 (vv. 18, 26), perhaps because she knew more than Aquila or had a more prominent role in correcting Apollos. But the fact that the biblical authors will only mention them together and will only say that "they" took Apollos aside and corrected him (v. 26), rather than just "she," suggests a co-mission together in their marriage.

The passage describes a strange situation. A godly and zealous teacher, Apollos was out publicly teaching and yet was ignorant of an important aspect of the faith—namely,

---

a. Act 18:1-2, 24-28.
b. v. 2.
c. Priscilla, along with Aquila, is also mentioned three times in Paul's letters, among the greetings: Rom 16:3; 1Co 16:19; 2Ti 4:19.

Christian baptism — and he had no oversight to correct him. Priscilla and Aquila needed to rise to the occasion. What is missing in the account is a description of Priscilla's teaching ministry. Luke gives us no indication that Priscilla is out teaching publicly or regularly in the church. We would expect that he would if she was, just as he does in describing Apollos's ministry. There is no Acts 18:26 reading something like, "And because she knew the way more accurately, Priscilla went out and preached in the synagogue," or "she went out and taught in the church."

Instead, her distinctive prominence in this action of correcting promoted a brother with whom, it seems, the couple had come into friendship. Gender asymmetry does not mean that a woman should never correct a guy on a point of doctrine, especially if he is ignorant about it. I am grateful myself to have had corrections in my own public speaking on occasion, from men and women. Apparently, Apollos was too. Priscilla acts to serve the mission, however she can. In promoting her Christian brother in his calling, she empowers the needed work of God. Can you do the same for your guy with the gifts God has given to you?

Why not start picturing this on your dates? *Do I like where he wants to go? Or do I have trouble visualizing myself in his goals? As I get to know him, do I respond, somewhere in the deep place in my gut, to his vision of life, the use of our gifts? Could I follow him if need be, as God says of His bride in our opening quotation, "in the wilderness?"ᵃ Do I see, or is he helping me to see, what I bring to the table? Can I help with the mission I see in him?* If you

---

a. Jer 2:1.

are not responding to these questions positively, this may not be the guy for you. If you cannot respond in this way to any guy, you may not be ready to date well.

The Beloved Power

Christ, showing us the Beloved in relation to the Promiser, is our paragon of femininity, especially in addressing the extreme affliction of the fall. When all went awry with the crown of creation, the mighty Executrix powered and performed the rescue operation of the Great Ruler of All.[a] The Beloved was commissioned by the Promiser,[b] came in His name,[c] and willingly took up the work. The Beloved did this by choosing to love us,[d] speaking the truth to us,[e] giving life blood for us,[f] achieving powerful forgiveness for us, lavishing grace upon us,[g] sealing us up safely with the Holy Spirit,[h] making us together a body,[i] purchasing an exorbitant inheritance for us,[j] and filling all things for us.[k] The Great Help-Meet made this plan of redemption a success,[l] and all of it was done out of love for the Promiser[m] in the aforementioned *pactum salutis*.

You similarly bring great powers to bear on a mission. You need to ask now on whose mission those powers

---

a. 1Co 15:24-26.
b. Joh 5:30.
c. Joh 5:43.
d. 2Th 2:13.
e. Joh 17:8.
f. Psa 40:6-7; Joh 10:18; Eph 1:7; Heb 10:5-6.
g. Eph 1:7-8.
h. Eph 1:13-14.
i. Eph 1:23.
j. Eph 1:11.
k. Eph 1:23.
l. Joh 17:4.
m. Psa 40:8; Joh 17:5; Heb 10:7.

should be brought to bear. Abigail, of whom we spoke earlier, committed all of her resources: loaves and wine and sheep and grain and raisins and two hundred fig cakes.[a] You might not have quite so many fig cakes, but you have some great gifts to empower.[b] Are you able to bring them to help him? Such questions may challenge your view of what your life is about. Do you have a guy who wants to do a great thing for God while you just want a white picket fence with 2.5 children? If so, do you need to assess your priorities in life? Sometimes God gives us dates where this challenge happens.

Mission Merging

Even with the right priorities, relying on a man to apprehend a mutual mission may be hard to imagine if you are not with a specific guy. Until that happens, your mission is your own. What are you doing now to advance Christ's Kingdom? If you can get a good sense of that, it can help you in dating decisions. Many girls have avoided improper matches because they could not share the projected mission. They didn't want to be a soldier's, or a politician's, or a farmer's wife. That is fair. But a wise woman cultivates her mission to flex for the future.

Some gifted women worry about being squashed by an overbearing guy. My close friend, Donna, put it to me this way: "If I sense that a guy is threatened by my intelligence, and might try to squash me, I back off. I am willing to sacrifice my career for children or a mission but not

a. 1Sa 25:18–20.
b. Rom 12:6; 1Co 12:4–7; 1Pe 4:10.

for a man who *needs* me to be unsuccessful. And not for a man who does not care about my flourishing." Donna is right to be wary. What I am advising is not flexing to feed insecurities but flexing for a man's divinely dispensed mission. A man who is truly after God's purpose rather than his own prestige will show that in himself to you, if you are looking for it. You can see it in your dates.

* * *

Theresa was shaken up after her difficult romance with Horace, the seminarian, in chapter 7. She went on some dates with a few guys but was hesitant to get serious. Then came the young professor, Henry, a nice catch. She had been in one of his classes, and he was a fun guy. Henry was also quite patient. He was ten years older and respectful of the teacher-student relationship. But he wrote Theresa every year after graduation, for seven years. After that, he started writing more frequently, and eventually asked if he could call her. A request for a date, of course, then followed. Theresa's family was thrilled with this guy, so Theresa went along with the dating idea. She got a little concerned about how often they argued and how differently they saw the world, but that flag of disagreement was not fundamental, she thought, so she decided to give it time. (Henry's parents, it turned out, fought all the time, so he thought that this was par for the course.) She also had the pressure of being later in her twenties, a time when many women wonder if it is going to happen for them. They dated for a year and a half.

Things were getting pretty serious when something happened that settled her mind about breaking up. They lived some distance apart, which, of course, created a strain on things. Henry filled out a job application for her for a job nearby him, thinking that this could solve their distance problem. One thing though: he did this without telling her. When she found out, and they had an argument about it, Theresa realized that Henry wasn't seeing her as she was. He had created an image of her in his mind that she just wasn't. That he thought that she could just walk away from her teaching so easily, without even a discussion, convinced her that he didn't really know her, and wasn't trying to.

Their two different views on the relationship collided painfully when Henry took Theresa out for a walk on the beach. The moment he brought forth the ring, dropped to one knee and, to Theresa's great dismay, proposed, she had to reply, "I'm so sorry, but no." There was quite a bit of hurt for both of them. But I can tell you one thing— not as much as if they had gotten married.

No, mission merging does not mean you being squashed, but it does mean, like Christ, you putting another first for a worthy goal. A better illustration comes to us in the story of St. George, in Edmund Spenser's 1590 breakaway blockbuster, *The Faerie Queene*, quoted in our chapter opening. The problem was a dragon, ravaging the countryside and leaving everyone in fear. But St. George's quest to kill it is not one he can handle alone. He needs the ever-present aid of Princess Una. The story is an allegorical adventure of a man (St. George) and the true Church (Una). St. George must kill the dragon, "a monster vile, whom God and man does hate," but much of the story ends up focusing on Una and her role as prophetess and pray-er of the operation. Our opening quotation relays a part of Una's inspiring call back from the despair of George's suicidal thoughts.

George is a believer. In fact, his first name is "The Red *Cross* Knight," but like many men, he starts out not knowing where his mission is. Una helps him find it. He sometimes wanders off the track, seduced by false directions. She uses her resources to aid him and keep him on the mission. When St. George finally fights the dragon, the dragon actually kills him, and he is taken up for dead. Una prays for him and he is healed to finish the job. Their journeys merge because they ultimately have the same goal: the destruction of the dragon. Is it like this with you and your date? Are you on the same journey?

In this Elizabethan tale, Una's parents represent Adam and Eve. She has been raised, in a way, through their faithfulness. In real life, Eve had certain gifts that Adam immediately recognized for the first work. Sure, an ox might be better for plowing a field, or a horse for hauling timber, but this bone of his bone presented a partnership that would multiply their efforts and bring everything needed for success.[a] This is the kind of story God wants for you.

How is it going to work for you? Often the husband's work supports the family. But sometimes a woman's career works out to provide the primary income source. I am an admiring friend of Austin and Nova, the couple who arose from one of the breakups back in chapter 1, for whom it worked out this other way. Nova

---

a. Ecc 4:9–11.

works as an executive in a software company, and Austin is a stay-at-home dad to their three little girls. I can tell you, because I know them well, that they focus all the more on gendered relationship in their home. This situation will never be the norm, as financial provision is one principal way a man secures a woman, and the nature of childbearing calls a mother's heart home. Multiple data sets show that, statistically, married mothers today still do more than twice as much housework, as usually understood, and spend twice the number of hours on childcare than do their husbands.[91] But the stay-at-home dad situation can work, and work well, if the Bible's priorities hold sway. Again, God is not asking the question as to who brings home the biggest paycheck. He is asking if you are both adopting the mission He gives you.

A Priestly Place

You have a right to know what is coming if you sign on to a dangerous or stressful mission. I include this note for you if your date is a pastor or a pastor-to-be. If he is going to be faithful, the work will be very tough. It is one of those occupations that is impossible to keep contained in the church employee alone. Even if a ministering man has a wife who is not active in the church, she automatically has a relation to the church and to what her husband must go through. If he has that kind of demanding calling and you accept him, you will have that kind of calling too. You cannot escape it.

The prophet Ezekiel leads the way to restoration after Old Testament Judah went into exile in Babylon. He presents the program, if the people repent, and forecasts

what is in store for them as they rebuild. It is clear that
Ezekiel is laying great responsibility on the priests. As he
describes the reconstitution of this prominent priesthood,
he revives a Levitical law about whom priests can marry.
He says that they cannot marry widows or divorcees from
other marriages, but only a heretofore unmarried woman
or a widow of another priest.[a] Why such a restriction?
This rule, executed on a large scale, created a special class
of women whose husbands were priests.[92] The status sustained a sorority of sorts in which, if you were a member,
you would be conferred with special recognition, responsibility, and, hopefully, training. It was a way of caring for
the wives of those carrying extra responsibility in caretak-
ing the kingdom of God.

   This rule is not directly applicable today, but it needs
a counterpart. I appreciate Ezekiel's intent because I see
that great need. One time a local group of churches in
my area created a seminar to serve pastors' wives. It was
a thoughtful thing to do by our denomination. They
wanted to give attention to these women, understanding
the unique problems of having a husband who was a
pastor. When the women got together, the very first thing
the leader did was ask all the women to refrain from col-
lapsing right away! She knew what was coming. Pastors'
wives are usually prime candidates for counseling because
of the difficulties they and their loved ones face. She
literally said, "Don't all break down at once!" This is an
example of the demands of an uncommon calling. Whatever your guy's, are you ready for it?

---

a. Eze 44:22.

Bigger Than the Both of Us

You are wise to think through the mission of this man in front of you, and what it will mean for you. This mission-mindedness must be part of any relationship thinking that you do. If your relationship is about itself, it will flounder. If it serves a greater purpose, it will flourish.

You might be wondering why this book makes children a consideration in our dating. Do children have to be part of our future? Our God entails Two Who are in passionate relation. From that union proceeds the Holy Spirit, Who is the Witness to the love. Though variously expressed, the conception of the Holy Spirit as "the bond of love" between the first two Members of the Trinity stretches back through the history of trinitarian theology to the church fathers. If you have wondered, while reading about the Trinity in this book, where the Holy Spirit was, this is where.

Standing in the analogy of gendered romantic love, we see the first two Persons. Their communion itself eternally produces a Third Person, who then proves, pervades, and promotes the agreement of the Two. That is in God. Again, *our families are not the exact same thing as the Trinity, but our imaging-generation most definitely speaks It.* As Paul put it in one of his trinitarian passages, every family on earth is named from the heavenly Father (with Christ dwelling and the Spirit strengthening).[a] Making families in imitation is one way we begin to be filled with God's love.[b] Therefore, when there are two human

a. Eph 3:14–17.
b. Eph 3:18–19.

persons made in the image of God who are in relationship, that image is played out in time, and their love should eventually overflow. In a marriage, usually, that is in children. That is why kids are important. As the prophet Isaiah put it, God didn't make the earth to be empty but to be inhabited.[a] From the union proceeds other people. The intergendered communion itself produces them. And, not surprisingly, they need your gendered parenting to prosper, adding to the body of Christ. So, your mission will likely include discipling children. You should figure that into the calculus of your future. How are you going to do it? How will children help in the mission?[b]

Perhaps you are wondering about whatever happened to poor Theresa, after she broke off with California cult-bound Horace and walked away from Professor Henry on the beach. Maybe you began doubting whether she should have set such a high standard with her "all for Christ" idea. Let me put your worries to rest. Theresa is older now, and considerably wiser. I recently attended her wedding. I expect she and her groom, Hal, to be very, very happy together, because they are so straight on what matters. Even with all the heartache involved, she looks back with gratitude to God from all those potential marriages from which she was preserved. Hal is the real catch, a man who truly is holding back nothing from the Lord. He has also been through a lot and has become a man after God's own heart. He wanted a woman with whom he can share a mission and found her in Theresa. When I last spoke to them, I could see little to add to their combined wisdom.

---

a. Isa 45:18.
b. Ecc 4:12.

On to Your Inevitable Wedding Day

For married love between man and woman is bigger than
oaths, guarded by right of nature.
— Aeschylus[93]

The being of the world and my own being,
the death He died so that my soul might live,
the hope of all the faithful, and mine too,
joined with the living truth mentioned before,
from that deep sea of false love rescued me
and set me on the right shore of true Love.
— Dante[94]

Answering the Question

It is hard doing a funeral. Funerals lug along a heaviness, even among the best of circumstances. But it is great doing a wedding. Even when occurring among the most trying of side stories involving friends or relatives, a wedding carries an exultant joy. The first ceremony means facing death. The second celebrates life. Yet there is something harder than funerals: telling an engaged couple that they shouldn't get married. It is excruciating. If you are a pastor, may you never have to face telling two people that you cannot, in good conscience, marry them. It is facing life and death at the same time. Maybe that is why I wrote this book, to help spare pastors everywhere this experience. Better for everyone, if you are the engaged or dating couple, that you figure it out yourselves. You now have the steady platform to figure it out. The ancient secret the Bible gives us is a reliable rock upon which you can make the decision. I have now given you (in Part II) three questions to ask about your date: *Can my date secure me / give me rest? Can my date take charge for me / esteem me? Can my date get the mission / empower our mission?* Asking these may eliminate many prospects. That's all right. Discrimination is the name of the dating game. You need more than just two arms to hold you or someone to be in bed with. You are in the neat time of life when you might fall in love with a person you don't know. If you do marry, for the rest of your life, you are called to fall in love each day with a person you *do* know, the person you married. The reason this book is appropriate for you and not for married people is that we need different advice for that next phase. Then we are no longer contestants in the quest. We become caretakers of vows. But now, you are in the realm of choice.

* * *

In the summer of 1989, I was deciding whether to ask my girlfriend to marry me. I had known her for six months. I was plagued with great doubts and uncertainty. So I stopped life and began fasting. I withdrew from contact with her and everyone else to just seek God alone about whether this one was *the* one. Looking back at how little I understood then, I feel like I could have easily made a bad decision. I was not wise enough to make the judgment. But I ended up making it this way. I came to a point in prayer when I felt like, when I visualized Mary K., I said, "At last, bone of my bone, flesh of my flesh." That is, I saw the beginnings of these gender principles discussed in this book already in operation. So I decided to go through with it. When you come to that same precipice, I pray that what you have read here may help you attain peace in making the dangerous decision.

The Bible is wise where we are not. These questions exploring the asymmetries of gender make for wise dating because the Persons of God underlie intergendered marriage, giving Christ to us as our paragon for both the masculine and the feminine. And because marriage begins in dating, these principles give us a reliable guide from the get-go.

The Jane Principle

In many areas of life besides dating, righteousness is a matter of repeated no-saying to bad alternatives, resisting the temptations to exit off the road stretching out in front of you. With enough of denying the wrong ways, the right way becomes clear.[a] It is also like this with your journey toward someone who could be *the* one. I call this the "Jane Principle," after the nineteenth-century novels by Jane Austen and *Jane Eyre* by Charlotte Brontë. The common moral in all these Jane books is waiting with integrity. The heroines bucked the cultural idol of a rich husband and turned down wealthy suitors who didn't meet certain standards. The books remain popular for

---

a. Mat 7:13-14; Jam 4:7.

their portrayal of a woman being strong, guarding the gold, being able to say no to a love that wasn't right. These Jane books are on to something. That is why we started *this* book with learning how to end before we begin.

This is not a book about how to get married, but about how to make the decision to marry. The fact is, you could do all the things I advise in all the preceding pages — even meeting the family! — and never end up at the altar. Because our lives are ruled by providence— that is, God's good governing of what comes to us and what does not[a] — there is no guarantee that, even if you want to get married, you will. If there are obstacles in you that are preventing it, the material of Part III of this book can help you address them. As you ask and answer: *Can I secure / give rest to my date? Can I take charge for / promote my date? Can I find our mission / empower our journey?*, you grow to a more eligible place.

But if you find no match, it does not mean that there is something wrong with you. You might remain single because God, in His great jealousy, does not want to share the treasure in you. Instead, He wants His jealousy personally to overcome your personal shame. While all the Jane books end happily in marriage,[95] there is no guarantee that making right decisions will end in marriage in real life. Jane Austen herself lived out that lesson. Though receiving proposals, she made the wise choice of not marrying rather than marrying just to marry. Consequently, she never married. But all this does not mean a life without love. For there is one guarantee that I can make to you.

---

a. Rom 8:28.

You Will Not Miss Out on a Wedding Day

One time, Jesus is teaching a group of people about God and a hush falls over the crowd. This is near the climax of Jesus's public teaching in Jerusalem. It comes after a long series of encounters[a] in which His disciples, and then other people, were asking Him all sorts of questions and He kept correcting them on the issues. "You misunderstand about taxes... misunderstand about children... misunderstand about marriage..." and so on. People were getting used to Him going after motives. Suddenly a man comes up to Him—a scribe, no less—and says something right to Jesus. This is a rare moment. Jesus looks at the scribe for a second and commends him. This has an awe-inspiring effect on the crowd. As I said, a hush falls. The narrator, Mark, concludes, "From then on, no one dared ask Him any more questions."[b]

What silences everybody? Something in the scribe's answer and Jesus's praise of it makes the people lose their stomach for questions. What is it? The scribe asks a simple question: Which of God's commandments in the Old Testament was the greatest of all?

> And one of the scribes came up and heard them disputing with one another, and seeing that he answered them well, asked him, "Which commandment is the most important of all?"

---

a. Mar 8–12.
b. Mar 12:28.

Jesus answered, "The most important is, 'Hear, O Israel: The Lord our God, the Lord is one. And you shall love the Lord your God with all your heart and with all your soul and with all your mind and with all your strength.' The second is this: 'You shall love your neighbor as yourself.' There is no other commandment greater than these."

And the scribe said to him, "You are right, Teacher. You have truly said that he is one, and there is no other besides him. And to love him with all the heart and with all the understanding and with all the strength, and to love one's neighbor as oneself, is much more than all whole burnt offerings and sacrifices."

And when Jesus saw that he answered wisely, he said to him, "You are not far from the kingdom of God."

And after that no one dared to ask him any more questions.[a]

We see the genius of Jesus's answer: other commands you could obey without thinking. You could obey those with your lips or your hands or feet, but not this one. This one takes your complete involvement. Fulfilling it presupposes affection between God and you. Jesus is saying, Do you want to go to the heart of the matter? Here it is: *God is Someone to be in love with.* Love with your heart, love with your soul. Love, love, love. It's about a love affair. Then they understand: Jesus considered God

---

a. Mar 12:28–34.

to be someone with whom you have a personal, vibrant, affectionate, adoring relationship. All religious wrangling comes down to a relationship with God. He is not a principle. He is not a political end. He is not a means of good conduct. And He is not far away.

Now, when Jesus says that, something ripples through the minds and hearts of the crowd. Something at last dawns on them. He has been getting at it and getting at it, through clearing the temple, and teaching different ways, and now it clicks. They realize that Jesus has this love affair. In the next moment, they must realize that they do not. Then they know that whatever issue they would raise, whatever question they would ask, whatever point they would argue, Jesus would bring it back to this. This is what He has been doing all along. At the heart of any issue is this matter of relationship with God. Do they love God? Do they know if God loved them? Do they know God? They do not. And that lack will be revealed in any discussion with Jesus Christ.

And from then on, no one dares to ask Him any question.

Jesus perceives that the scribe is "not far" because the guy has a hint about how a love for God comes about in people. The scribe notes how that love with God was more than "all whole burnt offerings and sacrifices"[a]—that is, the things we might do to get to God. The scribe doesn't say that those sacrifices meant nothing, nor that they were unimportant, just that they were getting at something beyond themselves. And this is

---

a. Mar 12:33.

what changes Jesus's gears and ends His criticism. Jesus recognizes that the scribe recognizes that the sacrifices *we* make cannot make love between us and God. Trying to love God ourselves cannot establish that love affair. Rather, accepting Jesus's sacrifice for us does it. He makes "the whole burnt offering," of which the scribe spoke, Himself for you. He supplies the love in the love affair. That is why you should wake up in the morning and want to be with Him. That is how He becomes your date. Who always shows up.

And this is how you are guaranteed a wedding day. If you allow Christ to supply this love, you will be in the real wedding, as a member of His bride. All our weddings are ramshackle make-believe in comparison to our union with Christ to which history is heading. Even if you "lose" the dating quest in not securing an earthly mate, He has made it so you will not miss out on the true marriage. In Christ, there is no missing out. For when God draws the analogy for us of the love in the Trinity, He is showing us our future, beginning in our present. We shall be caught up in the archetype of romance we see demonstrated between the great Promiser and the great Beloved. This should convince you of your worth, that you are a treasure worth guarding, and give you peace regarding your dating outcomes.

What a Good Match is Made Of

If the questions that apply to you from Parts II and III of this book feel overwhelming to try to answer, just let them stew around inside of you for a while. You'll get it.

Being masculine and being feminine doesn't mean doing everything right. You'll notice that many of the stories of this book are stories of people who didn't do everything right. But there are many stories of redemption. Gabriel proved that in a profound way to Lauralee in chapter 8. Nowadays Gabriel speaks gratefully of Lauralee who, he says, "considers me as patient even when I am not." If you are feeling like up to this point you have not done some things in the best way, that may be healthy conviction. If you have the Holy Spirit of God, you can change and start doing it right. God is very gracious to those who want to learn.

On my first date with Mary K., going ice-skating, we agreed to meet first at a diner. Mary K. had just rushed out of the shower to get there and hadn't paid much attention to how she looked. I greeted her by saying that she looked like a drowned rat. Yes, I really did say that. I wouldn't recommend following my example there, especially on a first date. It is kind of a wonder that we ended up married, considering how I started out. Honestly, neither of us was very invested in the relationship at that point, and we clearly were not trying to impress each other. In a funny way, that worked to our advantage. Once we actually spent time together and tried on the clothes of this book with one another, we were smitten—and still are.

Still, considering some of my behavior toward her when we were dating, it should be a surprise to you that my wife married me. But then, it is also a wonder that Jesus Christ died for me. I put the two in the same category: outrageously undeserved blessings from God. So as I say, all is not lost if you do not do everything right.

Remember that your dating really is a foreshadowing of your potential marriage. So I will let you in on a secret, before you get there. A good marriage is made of, not two people acting toward each other perfectly, but two people forgiving each other consistently.[a]

These things make dating an adventure in growth. As you date well, you will learn about life, yourself, and God. As you date with integrity, you will grow in your manhood or your womanliness, and so enrich all your close relationships, even the non-romantic ones. You have a lot going for you. In addition to this book's counsel, if you are in Christ, you have God's providence working for you all the time, powerfully ordering the circumstances for what you need in dating. You also have your particular gifts, which you can use in the quest to win an Achsah or an Othniel. And you have the Date that always shows up, Who has made His intentions for you quite clear. May all these guide and support you as you process toward the inevitable wedding day.

---

a. Eph 4:32.

Forty First-Date Questions

Nervous about what to talk about on the first date? Here are some suggestions if you suddenly cannot think of anything to say:

1. What animal would you see yourself as?
2. If you could travel anywhere in the world for free, where would you go?
3. What do you think of dating apps?
4. Can one believe in outer-space aliens as a Christian?
5. What is the biggest need you see in the Church?
6. What food would make you excited if you knew that you were having it for dinner?
7. Can you recall a super emotional moment, when you were really moved by something?
8. What games do you see yourself playing in twenty years?
9. If a friend showed you a tattoo design he or she was considering getting, how would you advise?
10. What do you think God has been trying to teach you recently? Are you learning it?
11. What do you love about where you live? What do you dislike about it?
12. When is Jesus coming back?
13. Tell me about your family. Are you close with them?

14. Can you think of a movie that should have ended differently?

15. If someone asked you to listen to them sing and then he/she couldn't really sing well, what would you say?

16. If you had a million dollars specifically to give away to some charity or ministry, which would it be?

17. Fiction or Nonfiction? Old or New movies? SciFi or RomCom? How come?

18. What makes you feel secure? / What gives you rest?

19. If you made a Bible passage the background for your phone, what passage would it be?

20. What is the most wonderful feeling in the world for you?

21. Where do your parents live?

22. As seventy percent of the earth's surface is under water, do you think we should explore it more?

23. Which is better, a church that has sound doctrine or a church that is really doing a great job in discipleship and outreach?

24. What is your most used non-work-related app on your phone?

25. What is a goal or dream you hope to achieve?

26. Deep down, do you think that Pluto should be recognized as a planet?

27. If God were to come down and tell us that He has decided to remove a chapter of the Bible, which chapter would you hope it was?

28. Is there another country you could see yourself living in?

29. What was a time when you couldn't stop laughing?

30. What was the subject of your last prayer?

31. If you have brothers or sisters, what is your birth order? How did it feel being first-born/last-born/in middle/an only child?

32. What is a topic you feel you could talk about endlessly?

33. If your life was the Wizard of Oz, when did it go from black and white into Technicolor©?

34. Is there something you remember that your closest friend said about you that shocked you?

35. What's something you see someone or some group doing now that gives you hope for the world?

36. Was there a situation you remember when you think you should have stepped forward more or been more active for something?

37. Who, not running now, would you want to elect to be president?

38. When you are at work, do you think that God smiles at the actual work that you are doing?

39. Who is someone that you would never ever ever want to be your next door neighbor?

40. If you and I were the last two people on earth, would you go on a second date with me?

An Entirely Inadequate Appendix II

The Trinity and Us

*The urgency of confuting heretics made it necessary to find
new words to express the ancient faith about God.*
— Thomas Aquinas [96]

*Whoever sees this even in part, or in a puzzling manner in a
mirror (1 Corinthians 13:12), should rejoice at knowing God....
Whoever does not see it should proceed in godliness toward
seeing it, not in blindness toward making objections to it.*
— Augustine [97]

Some of the talk about the Trinity in this book may appear
off the beaten path. I speak in a shorthand that I am writing
this post-note to explain. Unfortunately, there are two
types of person who might read this appendix. The first
type is just curious to learn more about the Trinity, and
perhaps further elucidation of Christian dating. I fear the
technical language will put him off. He will have little use
for all these theological trails and terms. The other type is
suspicious of my orthodoxy, wanting reassurance that I
am speaking of God aright. She will be unsatisfied with the
brevity of this account. Hence, I fear that no reader will, in
the end, be properly served. Nonetheless, I feel obliged to
offer some small explanation for the theological reasoning
that underlies the lessons in the text. For those wishing an
account properly justified and referenced, I have written a
different book, although unpublished as of this printing. It
is called *Splayed Out in Space and Time: Trinitarian Theology Unlocked Through the Priority of Relationship*, and it
renders a full treatment. I invite the curious to join me there

when it becomes available. But here, in brief, is where I am coming from, how I believe God has pulled back the veil for us, and how we pass through that veil to know our Creator.

Part I: Where I Am Coming From

I am writing about the Trinity from within a pro-Nicene, Western (that is, Constantinopolitan settlement), and Reformed tradition. This means that I believe that God is one. He is independent and self-existent. His essence is all absolute perfections in and of Himself, and all perfections relative to the creatures. With equal urgency, our one God is three Persons. They are coeternal and of one substance, coequal in power and glory. None is greater or less than the Other. Each Person possesses the full nature or all the qualities of the essence of God, and each One's substance is of Himself, *auto-theos*.

Furthermore, one of the Persons alone is not lesser than the Three together. The Trinity itself is as great as each Person in it, and each Person in it is as great as the Three together. Moreover, the distinct Persons are not separate from One Another. They mutually indwell One Another and have the same understanding and wisdom and one divine will. They operate inseparably—that is, harmonically—together in all the actions of God, even those which are properly appropriated to one of the Persons.

Yet they are distinct Persons Who are in relationship. This is the meaning of personhood, to be in relation to another person. And this is precisely how They are distinct: the Father of the Son, The Son of the Father, and the

Holy Spirit of the Father and the Son. The only distinction between the Persons is in mutual relations flowing from Their origins. The Father is of none, neither begotten nor proceeding. The Son is eternally begotten of the Father, and the Holy Spirit eternally proceeds from the Father and the Son. An ontological, irreversible and hypostatic taxis, or order, in the Trinity arises from these relations. Though, again, They are equal, yet the Father is the first in his innascibility (that is, incapable of being born) and paternity in relation to the Son. The Son is second in his filiation in relation to the Father. The Holy Spirit is third in His procession, in relation to Them in Their common spiration. And the Spirit's procession is qualitatively different than the Son's. We see the effects of this taxis, for example, in God's mission of redemption. The Father sends and operates through the Son. The Son acts for and reveals the Father. The Son from the Father sends and operates through the Spirit. The Spirit acts for and reveals the Father and Son together.

Part II: Pulling Back the Veil

No one has seen God, or can.[a] A great void veils from us Their union as the divine Persons. Their eternal processions dwell in unapproachable light.[b] But God has a great passion for us to know Him.[c] He sees our need to know ourselves through knowing Him. With marvelous benevolence to our creaturely poverty, God pulls back the veil of the Holy of Holies by way of analogy. He has decided

---

a. Exo 33:20; Joh 1:18; Joh 6:46.
b. 1Ti 6:16.
c. Joh 17:24.

to give us analogical knowledge of His true Self and, in
His Trinity, Their true Selves.

So He acts. What God is we know through what He
makes and does. His undertakings toward us and which
include us (creation, providence, redemption, glorifica-
tion) incessantly reveal His processions, as the historic,
ecumenical creeds labor to tell us.

These external works and missions reveal the Trinity's processions, or Their eternal, internal relations, and
they do so extensively and intensively; that is, God reveals
Who He is in His acts first generally. For example, the
Father eternally begets the Son, so in our space-time He
incarnates the Son,[a] born of a virgin. And They eternally
spirate the Holy Spirit, so in the mission They both send
the Holy Spirit upon us.[b] As well, we see Them in Their
particular acts, for example, in how Jesus breathes the
Spirit on the disciples[c] because something analogous to
that breathing goes on in eternity. The revelation of Their
processions, like the inspiration of the Word, is both
plenary (extensive) and verbal (intensive).

This correspondence gets God halfway there in His
communication of His Self to us. He completes the bridge
of our knowing Him in His analogizing in us. That we
might understand, He makes us in His image and calls
us to imitate Him in His works. In this mirror of our
own selves, we see Him through the glass darkly.[d] This
understanding explains why the Bible repeatedly tells us

a. Psa 2:7.
b. Joh 14:26; Joh 15:26.
c. Joh 20:22.
d. 1Co 13:12.

to imitate the relations of the Trinity, as perceived through the lens of God's actions. As the poem goes,

> *First it is in Trinity sung,*
> *Then it is in Their actions done.*
> *Then in Their image we become*
> *The holy, glimmering imitation!*

God is terribly bold in the written revelation with the human metaphors He uses for Himself. Yet His analogies are controlled and limited by His prescriptive will for us, as revealed in those same Scriptures. In this way, the Bible's commands constrain how we compare our experience with the Trinity.

Part III: Passing through the Veil

How are we in His image? While we may be in the image of God's essence as individuals through possession of His communicable attributes, or in His royal likeness as stewards of His kingdom on earth, the Bible tells us that we are in Their trinitarian image through our earthly relationships. While the relational analogy of Father and Son is prominent for us in the New Testament and heavily ingrained in subsequent theological history, it is not the only relationship God has given us, nor the only one the Bible's trinitarian descriptions use. Both Moses and Paul locate the trinitarian image in the intergendered union of marriage. Moses pictures the Trinity in the act of creating gender,[a] and Paul compares Christ both to a husband (in

---

a. Gen 1:26–28; Gen 2:18–24.

relation to His church[a]) and to a wife (in relation to the Fountainhead of the Trinity[b]), encouraging us to esteem Christ as our paragon in all things. Both women and men find themselves in Christ as they asymmetrically love each other. Many other passages follow suit to lead us to understand our families as a prime analogy of the Trinity.

Some may object, out of fear of assailing God's unity, to distinguishing the Persons in a way that informs our relationships. The concern is that by focusing on how the Persons love each Other in God's external quests, so reflecting Their ontological reality, we lose sight of Their perichoresis—that is, how They mutually indwell One Another. But Their Unity should never obscure Their distinction as Persons, just as Their inseparable operations—how the triune Persons are involved in every act of God—should never obscure Their distinct doings in creation and redemption. This book seeks to speak in a way that avoids *both* Arianism *and* Modalism—that is, to do just what the Athanasian Creed says to do: *not* divide the Substance of God *nor* confound the Persons of God.

To do human gender right, and to worship God aright, one needs to know that two-in-relationship is God's image. God has given us to worship and to learn to love each other genderly by apprehending how the image parallels God in His works. So, for example, theologians have struggled to distinguish the Persons of God, and it really can only be done through Their relations of origin to each Other. Likewise, people struggle to distinguish men and women from each other, and it really can only

---

a. Eph 5:22-33.
b. 1Co 11:3.

be done through their relationship to each other. Thus, the Bible doggedly resists listing innate qualities to define either gender or the individual hypostases (or subsistences of each Person) of God. Instead, we learn to distinguish Them in Their mission, carried out with each other.

All that the Persons distinctly do in our salvation, They are first doing for One Another. They act to save by making and keeping promises to One Another, a *pactum salutis* in the Reformed tradition. Our gender parallel is found in the calls to husband and wife acting for each other and with each other. In both cases, divine Persons and gender, they are defined for us by how they love each other.

Similarly, a taxis of asymmetry is certainly consistent with pro-Nicene heritage and, in my judgment, demanded by Scripture. Likewise, the Bible says that a husband and wife love each other differently. There is an asymmetrical headship and promotion that foster a couple's intimacy and fruitfulness, and that asymmetricality mirrors what we see go on in the acts of God, which in turn gives us glimpses of God in approachable light.

Thus, there is an archetype to which we can trace back all our gendered experiences and callings. When we start with God in our understanding, as revealed in the Scriptures, we arrive at His image in our relationships. We learn about our intergendered relationships, how to begin them and how to deepen them, from learning about Him. And, in turn, our experiences enrich our understanding of God and power our worship. All this is in store for us by learning to date well.

TABLE OF BIBLE BOOK ABBREVIATIONS

1Ch	1 Chronicles	Isa	Isaiah
1Co	1 Corinthians	Jer	Jeremiah
1Jo	1 John	Jam	James
1Ki	1 Kings	Jdg	Judges
1Pe	1 Peter	Job	Job
1Sa	1 Samuel	Joel	Joe
1Th	1 Thessalonians	Joh	John
1Ti	1 Timothy	Jon	Jonah
2Ch	2 Chronicles	Jos	Joshua
2Co	2 Corinthians	Jud	Jude
2Jo	2 John	Lam	Lamentations
2Ki	2 Kings	Lev	Leviticus
2Pe	2 Peter	Luk	Luke
2Sa	2 Samuel	Mal	Malachi
2Th	2 Thessalonians	Mar	Mark
2Ti	2 Timothy	Mat	Matthew
3Jo	3 John	Mic	Micah
Act	Acts	Nah	Nahum
Amo	Amos	Neh	Nehemiah
Col	Colossians	Num	Numbers
Dan	Daniel	Oba	Obadiah
Deu	Deuteronomy	Phi	Philippians
Ecc	Ecclesiastes	Phm	Philemon
Eph	Ephesians	Pro	Proverbs
Est	Esther	Psa	Psalms
Exo	Exodus	Rev	Revelation
Eze	Ezekiel	Rom	Romans
Ezr	Ezra	Rut	Ruth
Gal	Galatians	Sos	Song of Solomon
Gen	Genesis	Tiu	Titus
Hab	Habakkuk	Zec	Zechariah
Hag	Haggai	Zep	Zephaniah
Heb	Hebrews		
Hos	Hosea		

ENDNOTES

CHAPTER ONE

1. Paul Simon, "Fifty Ways to Leave Your Lover," track 4 on *Still Crazy After All These Years*. Columbia, 1975, vinyl album.

2. Christopher Ernest Pullen, "The consequences of retained lures on free swimming fish: physiological, behavioural and fitness perspectives," (master's thesis, Carleton University, 2013), iii, https://curve.carleton.ca/ce20574d-c177-48d3-bb34-5648ab013630. Fish are generally able to rid themselves of all lure types.

3. Many scholars take "my Father's house" in John 14:2 to mean the temple, but the temple does not fit as a place to add on rooms for living, nor does it fit the eschatological promise Jesus is making. Jesus says that He is going away—that includes away from Jerusalem and the temple—to prepare for them "rooms," for which John uses the term μοναί (*monai*). John makes clear what Jesus means by that with the word's only other use in the New Testament, 14:23, where in the singular it is universally translated "home."

4. "Young wives would live in the homes of their in-laws." J. Duncan M. Derrett, *Jesus's Audience: The Social and Psychological Environment in which He Worked* (New York: The Seabury Press, 1973). "The extended family often lived together in one house, including the father and the families of his married sons." "It was in the household of the groom's parents that the couple would begin its married life." S. Safrai and M. Stern, eds, *The Jewish People in the First Century: Historical Geography, Political History, Social Cultural and Religious Life and Institutions*, vol. 2 (Philadelphia: Fortress Press, 1976), 732, 753. Joachim Jeremias notes that even in the varied practices of modern Palestinian bridal custom, the one universal is the nocturnal procession and entry "into the house of the bridegroom's father." Joachim Jeremias, *The Parables of Jesus*, 2nd ed. (New York: Charles Scribner's Sons, 1972), 172–173, 174.

5. "It was common to add rooms or small structures to the roofs of houses... The most frequent reason was the expansion of a family; a newly married son customarily brought his wife to lie in the family house. The father would set aside a room within the house for the couple or build a marital house on the roof." Safrai and Stern, *The Jewish People in the First Century*, 731, 758, 760. The archaeology of ancient Israel's architecture confirms this process of successive adding on to the family home.

6. "The established custom was to hold the wedding in the house of the bridegroom or his parents. The bridegroom fetches the bride and brings her to his house, where the bridal table and chamber are ready." Joachim Jeremias, "νύμφη," in *Theological Dictionary of the New Testament*, eds. Gerhard Kittel and Gerhard Friedrich, trans. Geoffrey W. Bromiley (Grand Rapids: Eerdmans, 1967), 4:1100. "The bridegroom called for her at her house and led her... to his parents' house in a festal procession." A. W. Argyle, "Short Comment: Wedding Customs at the Time of Jesus," *Expository Times* 86, no. 7 (1974/1975): 215. This is confirmed in Rubin Zimmerman, "Das Hochzeitsritual im Jungfrauengleichnis: Sozialgeschichtliche Hintergründe zu Mt 25.1–15," *New Testament Studies* 48, no. 1 (2002): 48–70. The same picture is given by Alfred Edersheim, *The Life and Times of Jesus the Messiah* (Maclean, VA: Macdonald, 1988; orig. publ. 1883), 2.455.

7. Late Judaism was familiar with this line of thinking, interpreting YHWH in Deuteronomy 33:2 to be like a bridegroom coming with a torch to meet His bride, Israel. Jeremias, *The Parables of Jesus*, 172.

8. Michael L. Satlow, "Marriage and Divorce," in *The Oxford Handbook of Jewish Daily Life in Roman Palestine*, ed. Catherine Hezser (Oxford: Oxford University Press, 2010), 349–350. Safrai and Stern, *The Jewish People in the First Century*, 756.

9. Safrai and Stern, *The Jewish People in the First Century*, 756–757, 760.

10. Just consider a few of the metaphors Jesus goes on to use in the Gospel of John's farewell discourse. He casts the disciples as branches of Himself, a vine, while God the Father is a vinedresser (Joh 15:1–6). The Holy Spirit is made a legal paraclete or counselor (Joh 14:16; Joh 14:26; Joh 15:26; Joh 16:7). Throughout the evening, disciples become servants/slaves (Joh 15:20), friends (Joh 15:15) and pregnant women (Joh 16:21–22).

11. The dating of 1 Corinthians is important for seeing Paul's later relationship to Barnabas. Paul began his second missionary in AD 50, after the Jerusalem Council. The Corinthian correspondence and visits then probably took place in the years AD 55–56, some five years after the conflict. (Galatians also mentions Barnabas, but by my reckoning, Galatians was written earlier before the Jerusalem Council, and so also before the second missionary journey.)

CHAPTER TWO

12. George Lucas, *Star Wars* (Lucasfilm Ltd., 1977).

13. Spoken by Mrs. Malaprop to Lydia, Scene I, in Richard Brinsley Sheridan, *The Rivals: A Comedy*, originally published 1775, (A Public Domain Book-Kindle Ed., 2012), 14.

14. Paddy Chayefsky, *Marty* (Hecht-Lancaster Productions, 1955).

15. David H. Olson, John Defrain, and Amy K. Olson, *Building Relationships: Developing Skills for Life* (Minneapolis: Life Innovations, 1997), 49–52, for example, summarize the results of numerous studies.

16. "Why Remarry," *The New York Times*, December 19, 2010, https://www.nytimes.com/roomfordebate/2010/12/19/why-remarry reports on studies done by the Pew Research Center and the University of Virginia's National Marriage Project.

17. Sharon Sassler, "The Higher Risks of Cohabitation," *The New York Times*, December 20, 2010, https://www.nytimes.com/roomfordebate/2010/12/19/why-remarry/the-higher-risks-of-cohabitation.

18. Lisa A. Philips, "The Endless Breakup," *Psychology Today* 52, no. 3 (May/June 2019), 76, cites the research of Stanley and Rhoades.

19. Stephanie Coontz, *Marriage, a History: From Obedience to Intimacy or How Love Conquered Marriage* (New York: Viking, 2005), 296.

20. W. Bradford Wilcox, "Why the Ring Matters," *The New York Times*, December 19, 2010 (updated June 30, 2011), https://www.nytimes.com/roomfordebate/2010/12/19/why-remarry/why-the-ring-matters.

21. Nancy Pearcey, *Love Thy Body: Answering Hard Questions about Life and Sexuality* (Grand Rapids: Baker Books, 2018), 151, cites a ChristianMingle survey saying that 61 percent of self-identified Christian singles there were willing to have casual sex without being in love, 76 percent said sex did not require being in love, and 89 percent simply flat-out stated that they weren't willing to wait for marriage to have sex.

22. Pearcey, *Love Thy Body*, 127–129.

23. Othniel faced the foe called Cushan-Rishathaim, King of Aram Naharaim (Jdg 3:8, 10). Some scholars balk at this identification because the location name, the Hebrew equivalent of Mesopotamia, means this ruler hailed from a great distance. Others note the implication. This conqueror of faraway Canaan was an emperor of ancient Near East. The reach of his empire identifies Cushan as the most powerful enemy of the book of Judges, more powerful than the local neighbors the rest of the Israelite judges confronted. Daniel I. Block, *Judges, Ruth*, NAC 6 (Nashville, Broadman & Holman, 1999), 152. Cushan as the ultimate enemy comports with the book's pattern of things

starting out good, with the best, most accomplished judge, and ending with the least effective, Samson, who never once leads the tribes into battle.

CHAPTER THREE

24. Odysseus to Nausikaa, in Homer, *The Odyssey*, Book VI: 198–203, translated by Robert Fagles (New York: Penguin Books, 1996), 174.

25. The low divorce rates of arranged marriages are well known. For a recent popular canvasing, consider Ji Hyun Lee, "Modern Lessons From Arranged Marriages," *The New York Times*, January 18, 2013, https://www.nytimes.com/2013/01/20/fashion/weddings/parental-involvement-can-help-in-choosing-marriage-partners-experts-say.html. Olson, et. al., *Building Relationships*, 22, also point out how cultures with parent-arranged marriages have fewer divorces. One may still debate the reasons for this however.

26. Match Group, Inc., "Report on Form 10-K for the Fiscal Year ended December 31, 2018, https://s22.q4cdn.com/279430125/files/doc_financials/2018/annual/Match-Group-2018-Annual-Report-to-Stockholders_vF.pdf.

27. One passage in the Bible that *could be* construed as a description of innate qualities in woman is 1 Peter 3:1–7. I offer a better reading in Sam A. Andreades, *enGendered: God's Gift of Gender Difference in Relationship* (Bellingham, WA: Lexham Press, 2015), 101–102. The imagery of the book, Song of Songs, is another possible exception, but addressing it would involve a larger discussion of the use of the body pictures of the man and the woman in the song.

CHAPTER FOUR

28. Mitchell Davis was Vice President of the James Beard Foundation. These were his remarks at the New York University Food Studies Panel Discussion on Post Gender Food Writing (held March 3, 2011).

29. Gen 3:16 (NIV), with bracketed paraphrasing. Andreades, *enGendered*, 77, 111–112, discusses why this reading is likely.

30. Sam A. Andreades, *Splayed Out in Space and Time: Trinitarian Theology Unlocked Through the Priority of Relationship*, (forthcoming), "Marriage, The Image of God" with notes; and Andreades, enGendered, 210n1, cite theologians who agree with this three-fold categorization of explanations in the history of interpreting the *imago dei*. My explanation in the text is an elaboration of this basic historical categorization.

31. This is the preferred method of the Sumerian god Enki for creating a human.

32. So came Athena, from the head of Zeus: Pindar, *Olympian Ode* 7.33 in *The Loeb Classical Library*, ed. T. E. Page and W. H. D. Rouse, trans. Sir John Sandys (New York: The Macmillan Co., 1915), 74–75; Hesiod, *Theogony*, 924–929a, in *Theogony, Works and Days, Shield*, 2nd ed., trans. Apostolos N. Athanassakis (Baltimore: The John Hopkins University Press, 2004), 55.

33. Aristotle's view was that woman is a deformed, incomplete man, kind of like a first try. Aristotle, "Generation of Animals," in *The Complete Works of Aristotle: The Revised Oxford Translation*, ed. Jonathan Barnes, 2 vols., Bollingen Series 71:2 (Princeton, NJ: Princeton University Press, 1984–95), 1:728a, 2:737a. God apparently did better the second time with man.

34. Gregory of Nazianzus, "Theological Orations," in *Nicene and Post-Nicene Fathers*, 2nd series, vol. 7, reprint edition, eds. Philip Schaff and Henry Wace (Peabody, MA: Hendrickson, 1995), 321.

35. Andreades, *Splayed Out in Space and Time*, "God Created Gender to Speak Trinitarian Truths," with notes, gives references to the debate over a trinitarian reading of this verse.

36. The theology underlying this section and used hereafter in the book, and how pro-Nicene trinitarian theology can be expressed in marriage relationship terms, is summarized in the appendix and developed in Andreades, *Splayed Out in Space and Time*.

37. Paul Haggis, *Million Dollar Baby* (Warner Bros. Pictures, 2004). Clint Eastwood produced, directed, scored and starred in the film.

38. A recent excellent treatment is Brandon D. Crowe and Carl R. Trueman, eds., *The Essential Trinity: New Testament Foundations and Practical Relevance* (Downers Grove, IL: InterVarsity Press, 2016). This compact volume goes through the New Testament author by author, highlighting the Trinity in each.

39. I express in this sentence, in human relational terms, the doctrine of God's aseity or blessedness. Our Triune God is self-sufficient and content in Themself, as per Acts 17:25.

40. Paul explicitly relates gender to the creation story most prominently in 1 Corinthians 6:12–20; 1 Corinthians 11:2–16; 1 Corinthians 14:32–38; Ephesians 5:22–33; Colossians 1:15; Colossians 3:18–19; and 1 Timothy 2:8–15. Frank S. Thielman, "Ephesians," in. *Commentary on the New Testament Use of the Old Testament*, eds. G. K. Beale and D. A. Carson (Grand Rapids, MI: Baker Academic, 2007), 816, also recognizes an echo of Genesis 1:26 in Ephesians 1:20–23. Beale would further include Colossians 1:6–10 (G. K. Beale, "Colossians," in ibid., 843) and Colossians 3:9 (Ibid., 868) as well, to which implicit references could likely be added.

41. Andreades, *Splayed Out in Space and Time*, "The Missions Always Reveal the Processions Because God Passionately Desires Us to Know Him," elaborates on how God's missions always reveal His processions. Or, in modern parlance, the economic Trinity is always revealing the immanent Trinity.

42. By this statement, "What we do imitates what God does," I mean that the great movement of human lives to marry is there because the Persons of the Trinity enjoy the archetype of human marriage, as explained in Andreades, *Splayed Out in Space and Time*, "The Relational Image of God." God relates to us analogically, and we in relationship are the greatest analogy.

43. Anne P. Haas, Philip L. Rodgers, and Jody Herman, "Suicide Attempts Among Transgender and Gender Non-Conforming Adults: Findings of the National Transgender Discrimination Survey" (Williams Institute, UCLA School of Law, January, 2014). Earlier on, before silence on this matter was demanded, one could consider the candid comments of British researchers, for example in David Batty, "Sex changes are not effective, say researchers," *Guardian*, July 30, 2004, https://www.theguardian.com/society/2004/jul/30/health.mentalhealth. Time did not improve the results of outcome studies. In fact, a Swedish study found that those undergoing sex-reassignment surgery were nineteen times more likely than average to die by suicide, Cecilia Dhejne et al., "Long-Term Follow-Up of Transsexual Persons Undergoing Sex Reassignment Surgery: Cohort Study in Sweden," *PLoS ONE* 6, no. 2 (February 2011). After an initial euphoria, the gender dysphoric often find with time that the problems they thought they were solving by surgery still remain.

44. Andreades, *Splayed Out in Space and Time*, "How the Trinity Teaches Us Gender and Vice Versa."

45. Andreades, *Splayed Out in Space and Time*, "Stepping from Father and Son to Husband and Wife Adds Flashes of Divine Color."

46. If one travels across Turkey and visits the various museums of the towns of Anatolia, one can view what is perhaps the richest collection in the world

of remains from the period of the first-century Roman Empire, in statues, sarcophagi, grave stones, and decorative reliefs. In image after image of ordinary married women—*not* goddesses—from this time, one sees head coverings. The more the financial means of the woman, the more elaborate the covering. One may collect a veritable catalog of hooded head-covering styles from these artifacts.

47. Andreades, *enGendered*, 71–72, explains the reasoning of the firstborn principle. The asymmetry is then elaborated in chapters 9 and 10 of that book.

48. First Corinthians 14:34 instructs women to remain silent in church. The best way to understand Paul's statement here, in light of his earlier commendation of women praying and prophesying in church (1Co 11:2–5), is feminine silence during the time when prophecies are judged (1Co 14:29). That is, the women, along with unordained men, should refrain from stepping into the authoritative role of teaching given to the elders of the church, to which prophecies would be subject.

49. Andreades, *enGendered*, demonstrates and illustrates the principles at length. Really the dating questions in this book are an application of the ideas therein.

PART II
CHAPTER FIVE

50. Joyce Wadler, "The Lady Regrets: At Home with Renée Richards," *The New York Times* (February 1, 2007). In this article, Richards, a sex-change pioneer, was looking back thirty one years later, reiterating well-considered feelings from an interview eight years earlier: "I wish that there could have been an alternative way...If there was a drug that I have could have taken...I would have been better off staying the way I was—as a totally intact person...a man...I don't want anyone to hold me out as an example to follow...I'm not as fulfilled as I dreamed of being." Renée Richards Views Her Sex Change from Both Sides Now," *People Magazine* (March 15, 1999), 281–282.

51. John Milton, *Paradise Lost* Book IX: 886, 896–899, ed. Gordon Teskey (New York: W.W.Norton & Company, Inc., 2005), 221.

52. The fact that this passage came to be understood as a Messianic prophecy is key for understanding its New Testament interpretation as an exchange between members of the Trinity, and thereby showing us the relation to which our marriages are an analogy. The Dead Sea Scroll 11Q13 shows this Messianic interpretation of Psalm 110. The Testament of the Twelve Patriarchs: The Testament of Job 33:3 and the Talmud, b. Sanhedrin 38b, confirm it.

53. Of the 118 instances of *pa-am*, 110 mean "time." The others mean "foot" or "step."

CHAPTER SIX

54. Samuel A. Andreades, "Does She Matter? Emotional Intimacy in Marriage in Light of Gender Distinction" A Dissertation in Fulfillment of the Requirements for the degree of Doctor of Ministry (St. Louis, MO: Covenant Theological Seminary, 2013), 106.

55. This quote is universally attributed to Olympia Brown, but I have been unable to locate its origin. I have combed her principal works: *Autobiography, Democratic Ideals and Acquaintances, Old and New, Among Reformers*, which are interesting but do not contain it.

56. Evidence for priestesses appear in Egypt, Mesopotamia, and even Sidon (which was right next door to Israel), from the third millennium B.C. forward. But not only is there no evidence for such in Israel, there is counter evidence in the Bible.

57. Glenn Stanton, *Why Marriage Matters* (Colorado Springs: Piñon Press, 1997), 41–47, with notes on 192–193, especially note 56, gathers the data from studies up to the 1990s. Conservative Protestant women were the most sexually satisfied of any group studied. Pearcey, *Love Thy Body*, 130, confirms that "the people who are happiest sexually are married, middle-aged conservative Christians."

58. There is glorifying in turn to these many biblical expressions of the inter-trinitarian praise. The Father lifts the Christ up (Phi 2:9–10), which serves, in the end to glorify the Father (Phi 2:11).

59. Some Old Testament references to the glory of God, like the wisdom of God, suggest a Person. The New Testament describes the Beloved as "the radiance of God's glory" (Heb 1:3).

CHAPTER SEVEN

60. "Man or Muppet," Jason Segel, Nicholas Stoller *The Muppets* (Walt Disney Pictures & Mandeville Films, 2011).

61. J.R.R. Tolkien, *The Lord of the Rings-The Return of the King*: Book V, Chapter VI: The Battle of the Pelennor Fields (Ithaca, NY: Houghton Mifflin, 1993), 822–823.

62. Elizabeth Bernstein, "When You Can't Stop Competing With Your Spouse," *Wall Street Journal*, July 30, 2018, https://www.wsj.com/articles/when-you-cant-stop-competing-with-your-spouse-1532956525.

63. Tim Geiger, "How Can the Church Love Those Who Struggle With Same-Sex Attraction" (Harvest USA), https://harvestusa.org/how-can-the-church-love-those-who-struggle-with-same-sex-attractions/#.YEfP-I1Khqv, recounts the Barna Group statistics.

64. Samuel L. Perry and Cyrus J. Schleifer, "Till Porn Do Us Part? Longitudnal Effects of Pornography Use on Marriage Outcomes," *The Journal of Sexual Research* 55, no. 3 (March-April 2018): 284–296; Simone Kühn and Jürgen Gallinat, "Brain Structure and Functional Connectivity Associated with Pornography Consumption: The Brain on Porn," *JAMA Psychiatry* 71, no. 7 (July, 2014): 827–834.

65. Melissa C. Mercado et. al., "Trends in Emergency Department Visits for Nonfatal Self-inflicted Injuries Among Youth Aged 10 to 24 Years in the United States, 2001-2015," *Journal of the American Medical Association* 318, no. 19 (November 2017): 1931–1933.

66. In 1 Corinthians 7:39, the apostle Paul addresses the situation of a widow wishing to remarry, requiring that she only marry "in the Lord," meaning to another Christian. From this we can deduce that he would give the same instruction for a first time marry-er. But it is not a matter of just one verse. This Scripture (to which some add 2Co 6:14) follows upon a long history of restricting marriage of those in the covenant community to like members.

67. The author of Hebrews, though anonymous, is a man. Hebrews 11:32's self-referential statement uses the masculine form (διηγούμενον, *diēgoumenon*).

68. Andreades, *enGendered*, 76.

69. Herodotus, Xenophon, and even the conqueror himself, in fact, report that a feast and revelry was in progress when Cyrus's army captured Babylon. There is striking concordance between what is pictured in Daniel 5 and other historical sources on the city's fall.

70. The oddities of Esther gave it a harder road into the canon. Then, early in the Reformed tradition, Martin Luther denounced it and John Calvin never preached on or commented on it.

71. In regard to Esther's actions in Esther 2, I am following Karen Jobes analysis in Karen H. Jobes, *The NIV Application Commentary: Esther* (Grand Rapids, MI: Zondervan, 1999), 110f.

INTERLUDE

72. Elizabeth, in Jane Austin, *Pride and Prejudice*, eds. Donald Gray and Mary A. Favret, Fourth Edition (New York: W.W. Norton & Company, 2016), 71–73.

73. Victor Colicchio, Michael Imperioli, Spike Lee, *Summer of Sam* (Touchstone Pictures & 40 Acres and a Mule Filmworks, 1999).

74. Andreades, *Splayed Out in Space and Time*, "The Imitation of Trinitarian Relations,", explains how, based on Ephesians 3:14–19, our human families imitate the Trinity.

PART III
CHAPTER EIGHT

75. The word for "man" in Isaiah 32:2 is the gender specific 'Ish' (אִישׁ).

76. Daniel Johansson, "The Trinity and the Gospel of Mark," in Crowe and Trueman, *The Essential Trinity*, 50, explains these three scenes well as expressions of the Trinity.

77. Andreades, *enGendered*, 106, cites a number of survey sources showing that women's subjective well-being has declined over most of the industrialized world, measured since the 1970s.

78. In a 2010 telephone survey of 9,000 random women across the US, found one in five reported having suffered a rape or attempted rape at some point in their lives. There are limitations in the methodology of the study, but it could indicate a larger than realized rate of sexual assault. "Statistics," National Sexual Violence Resource Center, https://www.nsvrc.org/statistics.

79. Andreades, *enGendered*, 85–86, 114, 126, 127, explicates the Achsah story.

80. The examples given here are developed in Andreades, *Splayed Out in Space and Time*, "Footstool Securing and Footrest Making Mirror the Asymmetry of Origin."

81. "Modern Parenthood: Roles of Moms and Dads Converge as They Balance Work and Family," Social and Demographic Trends, Pew Research Center, March 14, 2013, https://www.pewresearch.org/social-trends/2013/03/14/modern-parenthood-roles-of-moms-and-dads-converge-as-they-balance-work-and-family/.

CHAPTER NINE

82. Aeschylus, *Agamemnon* 896–898 (The Complete Greek Tragedies, Volume I, translated by Richmond Lattimore, (Chicago: The University of Chicago Press, 1953), 62.

83. God as a Unity or a Member of the Trinity is represented by the feminine in the following Scriptures: God as mother (Isa 66:1–24, especially vv. 7–13); God "giving birth to" the mountains and the world (Psa 90:2), and to Israel (Deu 32:18), begetting the Son from the womb (Psa 110:3 LXX), or crying out in labor (Isa 42:1–25, especially vv. 13–15); God as a woman in a parable (Luk 15:8–10); Christ as a mother hen (Mat 23:37–39; Luk 13:34–35); and, if the second Member of the Trinity is to be identified with the feminine character of Proverbs, as Woman Wisdom (Pro 1:20–33; Pro 3:13–26; Pro 4:5–13; Pro 8–9), which Christ applies to Himself (Luk 7:34–35, consider also 1Co 1:24). The first name for Himself that God gives to the Patriarchs, El Shaddai, is blatantly feminine, as explained in Andreades, *Splayed out in Space and*

Time, "The Relational Image of God." This divine title appears over forty times. And the jealous love of a woman is the very flame of the Lord (Sos 8:6).

84. C. S. Lewis, *That Hideous Strength* (New York: Scribner, 1996), 316.

85. The General Social Survey (GSS), the National Survey of Families and Households (NSFH), and the Survey of Adults and Youth (SAY), reported in W. Bradford Wilcox, *Soft Patriarchs, New Men: How Christianity Shapes Fathers and Husbands* (Chicago: The University of Chicago Press, 2004) 207, 213.

86. The noun form πραΰτης (prautēs) is used another twelve times in the New Testament, sometimes translated as "gentleness."

87. Andreades, *enGendered*, 59, with accompanying notes, documents this female difference.

88. Lisa Diamond, "Sexual Fluidity in Males and Females," *Current Sexual Health Reports* 8, no. 4 (December 2016): 249–256. Stanton L. Jones and Mark A. Yarhouse, *Ex-Gays? A Longitudinal Study of Religiously Mediated Change in Sexual Orientation* (Downers Grove, IL: InterVarsity Press, 2007), 78, 94. Several dozen studies on change in what is called "orientation" were published in the 1950s through 1970s, but serious research disappeared when the *Diagnostic and Statistical Manual* removed homosexuality as a disorder from its pages in 1973.

89. A recent summary of the Harvard Medical School's Study of Adult Development may be found in Liz Mineo, "Good genes are nice, but joy is better," *Harvard Gazette*, April 11, 2017, https://news.harvard.edu/gazette/story/2017/04/over-nearly-80-years-harvard-study-has-been-showing-how-to-live-a-healthy-and-happy-life/.

CHAPTER TEN

90. Princess Una's upbraiding of the Red Cross Knight, in Roy Maynard, ed., *Fierce Wars and Faithful Loves: Book I of Edmund Spenser's The Faerie Queene* (Moscow, ID: Canon Press, 1999; orig. pub. 1590), 177–178.

91. Brad Wilcox gives a good rundown of household trends in W. Bradford Wilcox, "Surprisingly, Most Married Families Today Tilt Neo-Traditional," *Institute for Family Studies*, February 26, 2014, https://ifstudies.org/blog/the-real-modern-family-surprisingly-most-married-families-to-day-tilt-neo-traditional. But this is housework, as the text says, "as usually understood." We should bear in mind that what is often included in tallies of housework does not include important house-supporting tasks like filing income taxes, managing financial tasks, or fixing the car.

92. Ezekiel's concern for priests' marriages is also why marriage within the tribe for priests is emphasized in the Talmud, e.g. Lev 21:14–15, Lev 22:12–13. The comment in Safrai and Stern, *The Jewish People in the First Century*, 754, is helpful.

CONCLUSION

93. Apollo to the Furies, in Aeschylus, *The Eumenides* 217–219 (The Complete Greek Tragedies, Volume I, translated by Richmond Lattimore, (Chicago: The University of Chicago Press, 1953), 142.

94. Dante, Paradiso Canto 26: 58–63, *The Divine Comedy, Volume 3: Paradise* (New York: Penguin Classics, 1986), 308.

95. My wife points out that the Brontë novel *Vilette* does not have a happy ending because the guy dies, but no one reads this one.

AN ENTIRELY INADEQUATE APPENDIX II

96. Thomas Aquinas says this in Question 29, Article3, about the use of the word, "person," to describe the hypostases of God, Saint Thomas Aquinas, *Suma Theologiae Prima Pars, 1–49* (*Latin/English Edition of the Works of St. Thomas Aquinas*), edited by John Mortensen and Enrique Alarcon, translated by Fr. Laurence Shapcote, (Lander, Wyoming: The Aquinas Institute for the Study of Sacred Doctrine, 2012) Vol. 13, 312.

97. Augustine, *The Trinity-De Trinitate*, Book VI Chapter XI (par 10/12) Second Edition, tr. Edmund Hill (New York: New City Press, 2015), 264–265.